ADVANCE
THE AUDIT PRINCIPLE

"Jane Ann Craig is living proof that what looks like the worst thing can somehow be the best thing.

I can't wait for you to read her new book, *The AUDIT Principle*. You will hear the unbelievable story of a single mom, with cancer who went from likely failure to multimillion-dollar success…and how the turning point was an industry audit. The principles she learned on this journey worked beyond her wildest dreams, and she shows how they will work for you too. More than a story, the book is practical, inspiring, and honest. Jane Ann specifically show you steps to take to align your life with the laws of success. A great read, an even better tool for an exciting future."

— **JOHN MASON**, Author of *An Enemy Called Average* and numerous other national bestselling books

---

"I first met Jane Ann when she was facing what appeared to be unsurmountable odds. Thankfully she didn't give up. Instead Jane Ann created a system that took her from where she was to where she wanted to be. Jane Ann's five simple steps in *The AUDIT Principle* teach a time-tested process guaranteed to align your actions with personal power principles that will help you redefine what's possible and achieve a level beyond success."

— **DAN CLARK**, *New York Times* Bestselling Author and primary contributing author to the *Chicken Soup for the Soul* series

"There is no shortcut to success. But Jane Ann Craig lays out simple steps to put any person on a path from vision to victory. Her perseverance is the stuff heroes are made of—and with The Audit Principle, we can learn from her strategies. She gives readers tools to overcome obstacles and then inspires all to navigate to their own destinations of success."

— JODI ORGILL BROWN, Business Owner and
Award-winning Author

"Jane Ann's book is a guide to a bigger, bolder and better life. It is a fantastic read that led me through personal aha moments, giving me immediate insight and clarity on issues I had been wrestling with. As she speaks with you through every page and chapter you will feel understood, heard and empowered. But most of all she will wrap you in a blanket of clarity. And THAT clarity will bring so much new opportunity and joy to your life, I promise."

– TROY DUNN, The Locator

"Jane Ann Craig is truly a remarkable woman and a great mentor to all that know her. I am so glad she is sharing her inspirational story and confident that the steps in *The AUDIT Principle* will instigate great change in the lives of all who read it."

– CHRISTY TRIBE, CEO of Junior Achievement of Utah

The
AUDIT
PRINCIPLE

The AUDIT PRINCIPLE

5 POWERFUL STEPS TO ALIGN YOUR LIFE
WITH THE LAW OF SUCCESS

JANE ANN CRAIG

SHIPWAY
PRESS

Published in the United States by
Shipway Press, LLC
7984 South 1300 East
Sandy, Utah 84094

Book cover and interior design by
Francine Eden Platt • Eden Graphics, Inc.

Library of Congress Control Number: Pending

978-1-7327291-0-0   Paperback
978-1-7327291-1-7   ePub

Printed in the United States of America

10 9 8 7 6 5 4 3 2 1

This book is dedicated:

To Mom and Dad who loved me unconditionally and gave me every advantage possible. Thank you for always being proud and believing in me.

To my brother Bob, who has always been there. Life is a much greater adventure with you.

To David. We were an unlikely pair, the biker and the business woman. Thank you for giving me the best gift ever, our son Jonny. Your life was cut too short but every minute we had together was an adventure and your impact continues to live on.

To Mark. Thank you for pursuing and not giving up on me! You stepped into our lives at the perfect time. You continue to amaze me everyday with your love, patience and support. Love you, Babe.

To Jonny, there are not enough adjectives to describe the man that you've become. You are intelligent, witty, wise, gentle and generous. I'm so proud of you.

TABLE OF CONTENTS

FOREWORD

STORIES ARE POWERFUL, and good stories even more so, because they have the ability to move us, upend our perspectives, shape our attitudes, and inspire us to action. When I was young, my mom introduced me to JRR Tolkien by reading me *The Hobbit* on road trips. As an adult, I still love Tolkien, and I think that's because of what Tolkien called the "deep magic" of stories, which is a way of describing the power stories have to change the world. In a different but similar way, this book has a "deep magic" to it. Meaning, there is no way you read it and leave unchanged or walk away uninspired—this is too good a story for that. Though, I may be a little biased because my mom, the one who first introduced me to good stories, is Jane Ann Craig, and this story you're about to read is her story, our story.

My mom has always been the best storyteller. I loved traveling with her because she would fill the slow times with exotic tales of faraway places and amazing people. Little did I realize that we were, at the very same time, living a grand adventure of our own. With age comes perspective and the ability to understand the gravity of our lives and the courage it took to lead, take risks, and make something truly beautiful of it all. What I understand now is that my mom was writing her story in the midst of struggle and hardship. A story that has enabled and inspired me to also a write a story worth telling, and that's what I think you'll get from reading this book: a new inspiration and power to go out and write your own story.

In some ways it's a weird thing to introduce your mom and her book to the world. It's an honor but also a strange pressure. How do I tell the story without giving away what you're about to read? What stories do I tell? How much of our personal lives do I reveal? As I was thinking all this through, I thought of two memories that aren't included in the book but get at who my mom is and why this book matters. Both stories are simple, but they mean the world to me. The first memory is of seeing "The Lion King" eight different times in theaters. Eight times! "The Lion King" is a great movie, but there is no way today I could watch it eight times in a row. But my mom did. She was busy starting a company and providing for our family, and yet she made time to see a kid's movie with me eight times. The second memory is similar. There was a stage in our life where my mom had to travel a lot and work long hours. But before she would head off for the day, she would wake me up, place me on her lap, and eat a slow breakfast on the front balcony. I don't remember what we talked about, but I remember feeling known and loved.

These memories may not seem like a big deal, but they are to me, and they represent so much of who my mom is and why she did what she did, which was me. My mom worked hard, endured struggle, and took risks because she wanted to create a life *with* me, not simply for me. She wanted to attend my basketball games, see my plays, meet my friends, vet my girlfriends, take me on adventures, and do normal everyday mom stuff with me. That's why this book matters to me. It's her story of accomplishing something extraordinary in order to do something ordinary, be my mom. Which really is extraordinary.

As my mom was writing this book, I was opening a local business in Salt Lake City, Utah. I've always felt that there was something special about the two projects coinciding. My mom has a legacy of starting businesses, creating opportunities, mentoring young people, and blessing the world around her. As she was writing that story down, I was taking the lessons I learned from her and putting them into practice. To me, that's evidence proving the power of what she writes about. And sure, I am biased, but I am also not alone. Our community is filled with people who have gained a vision for their lives and the tools they needed to change the world from my mom.

I don't know where you are in life, I don't know what your dreams are, and I can't imagine the struggle you've experienced or the hard work you've already done. But what I do know is that you need to read this book because no matter where you are, it will inspire you and help you get to where you want to go. I think that's the most beautiful part of all. This book isn't for the elite, the super smart, or the incredibly gifted. It's for people like me. Ordinary people who need and want to do extraordinary things. People who want to write a good story with their lives.

A Proud Son,
JONATHAN MORRISON

INTRODUCTION

Six years into building my company, I received the call that our company was going to be audited. Not an IRS audit limited to our financial and accounting processes, but a regulatory audit that would include every aspect of our business. The audit period would include the start-up years of the company.

I started my company at the age of thirty-nine as a widowed single mom of a son just entering kindergarten. I had never started a company from scratch, raised capital, or held an executive management position before. Here I was leading a growing organization with offices and employees in two states and shareholders and partners. And we were being audited.

A life-changing principle revealed itself to me as I was preparing for our audit. I now understand it to be a universal law that has paved the way for every success and transformation I've experienced in my life. I call this law the AUDIT Principle.

This book is written with two goals in mind: to inspire you and to give you the actual steps needed for your transformation. Whether you are pursuing a corporate goal or a lifelong dream, a transformation is required. As they say in baseball, you can't get to first base without leaving home plate. Change is necessary to move from where you are to where you ultimately want to be.

The first part of this book is my story. I never imagined I would share my struggles. But this is what I have discovered: people are more inspired by our struggles and how we overcome them than by the actual success we achieve. Many times, the inspiration comes in achieving success because of our shortcomings.

So my goal in putting my life "out there" is to inspire you. If I can overcome adversity and accomplish extraordinary successes with my limitations, poor decisions, and hang-ups, imagine what you can do?

The second part of this book is the "How." It is the "How to apply the AUDIT Principle in your life," or, as I've told thousands of people, "How to achieve your goals, dreams, and visions."

This book is written for the person or organization that is dissatisfied with the status quo. It's for the reader who feels stuck and ready to move on to a higher level of productivity, achievement, and living. I'm sharing The AUDIT Principle with every person who is ready to live more abundantly, contribute more generously, and make the difference you were created to make.

Reading this book will give you the steps and the road map to leave where you are and move to a new and more magnificent destination.

1

THE AUDIT

"JANE ANN, ARE YOU SITTING DOWN?"

IT WAS JUST TWO SHORT WEEKS until Christmas, and I was spending my last workday of the year in my office clearing the clutter off my desk. I was looking forward to a little downtime at the end of the year to take a deep breath, celebrate the Christmas season with my family, and recharge my mental and emotional batteries. This would allow me to come back in January with a whole new perspective, full of the optimism that always accompanies the launch of a new year.

I had one last task on my "To Do" list for the year. I needed to write my annual Christmas/New Year's letter to my employees and shareholders. This had become a tradition for me. I wanted to make sure that all the great people who had stood with me and worked so hard the previous year knew how much I appreciated them. This letter in particular excited me. It had been one of the most successful years in our insurance company's history, and I was eager to share the news with my team.

Even now, many of my staff were still scattered throughout the state, scrambling to close last-minute year-end sales. As the head of the company, I knew it was important to show my appreciation for their efforts.

The other purpose of the letter was to cast both my vision for the company and my strategy for the upcoming year.

I made sure I was comfortable at my desk. The clutter had been cleared away, and I had a fresh cup of hot herbal tea close by with soft classical music playing in the background. The environment was perfect for letting the creative side of my brain engage and letting the words begin to flow.

I was just reaching for a sip of tea when the phone rang. It was Bob, our company Chief Financial Officer (CFO). By the tone of his voice, he wasn't calling with a cheery Christmas greeting. In addition to being my CFO, Bob was also my older brother. The inflection and tone of his voice was alarming.

"Jane Ann, are you sitting down?" he asked.

Trying to keep things light, I said, "I'm at my desk." I might have sounded like I hadn't a care in the world, but something about his voice had set my stomach on edge. My first thought was that a family member had been in a serious accident.

But then I heard the words no Chief Executive Officer (CEO) wants to hear: "We've received an audit notification."

My heart sank. So much for a quiet, reflective year-end vacation.

Bob went on to read a few government codes, statutes, and legalese from the notice we'd been sent. My mind was spinning with everything we were going to have to do.

His voice broke through the fog in my head. "Jane Ann, this isn't an IRS audit. This is an extensive regulatory audit. These guys mean business, and they're going to do much more than just spend a couple of hours in the office going over our books. They're going to review our entire organization. They will dig into everything we do!"

Bob's trepidation was contagious, and I felt the tension collecting between my shoulder blades. The peaceful environment dissipated. The clean desk, the classical music, and the hot cup of tea no longer mattered.

I heard Bob say, "Hello? Jane Ann?"

It had taken me so long to respond that he thought we'd been disconnected. I was still trying to regain control of my emotions. I responded with more confidence than I felt.

"No problem, Bob. We can handle an audit, but the timing is pretty tough for us. Can you request a delay in light of the holidays?" With so much of my team scattered, I knew it would be quite a feat to gather the troops before the holidays. I would need their help collecting the information the auditors would be asking for.

Although my words were confident and calm, I was genuinely concerned. An audit of any kind is an arduous process where your business is laid open for all to see. The examiners are paid to discover your deficiencies, and they're meticulous and efficient in their work, going through even the smallest details with a fine-tooth comb. In my grim mood, I imagined them taking joy in shining a bright light on every area of my company, bringing all our shortcomings, even though innocent, out into the open. I knew from stories I'd heard from other CEOs that there could be significant and costly consequences for any mistakes that might come to light.

As I hung up the phone from talking with Bob, another voice slipped into my consciousness. My attorney, who had become a good friend throughout the course of building my business, once told me, "Jane Ann, there are good people incarcerated at the Point of the Mountain [Utah's prison] due to poor judgment and technicalities." I knew the audit would be merciless, not caring at all for the things I had meant to do or wanted to do. An audit only reveals what is actually done, with no emotion or feeling involved.

A JOURNEY OF FAITH . . . AND STRESS

This was big. My stomach was churning. The consequences for failing an audit were daunting. As the CEO and founder of the company, I would personally be held accountable if the audit turned up any problems or discrepancies.

There's no good time for an audit, but this was a particularly difficult time for us. While we had just wrapped up a successful year, we were still scrambling. This business was a startup, and we operated with very little margin. Every day brought more than its share of challenges and stress.

Cash flow was especially tight, and once again I found myself in the challenging spot of trying to figure out how we were going to cover expenses and make payroll. Since it was December, I had to stretch things even further than normal to make sure we could pay our employees their well-deserved Christmas bonuses.

Starting a company is a journey of faith with very few

certainties. But failure was not an option. Shareholders invested in my company trusted me to bring them a return. Employees relied on me for their monthly paycheck. My young son depended on me. I felt the weight of all these expectations on my shoulders.

Because of the consistent financial reports from Bob, I knew that without a change in cashflow, we would likely be forced to close the company. But even with all those things gnawing at my mind, I had an inner peace. Despite the dire warnings and the red ink on the financial statements, I was confident that we'd see things through to the end and finish strong. I was convinced that my startup company would not only survive, we would achieve our ultimate goal, which was to celebrate a profitable acquisition.

With an unwavering certainty, rooted in faith, I set my mind on the things I knew to be true. I was fulfilling the call on my life. I was doing more than just going to work every day for a company I founded. I was walking out my unfolding destiny. I knew when I began that it wouldn't be easy. I was driven to conquer the obstacles and challenges.

DAVID VS. GOLIATH

To me this was an epic narrative, just like David and Goliath. In my story, I played the part of David, but instead of a shepherd boy with a few stones in his bag, I was a single mom with no experience in running a company. I was facing a massive giant, Goliath, who was a cold and uncaring corporate world.

As I sat at my desk that day, I couldn't help but think about both the obstacles and successes my company was facing. It takes money to make money, and the company simply didn't have any to spare.

Our sales were on the increase, and that was a good thing. Sales mean success. But every new sale also brought new pressures. From the time the contracts were signed, our new clients expected us to fulfill our promise of excellent and timely service. The problem was that the cash from those new sales wouldn't hit our books until invoices were generated, mailed, received, and paid.

It was my job to keep morale high among the team by celebrating even the smallest sales successes. It was also my job to exhort them to stretch our resources to the limit to make sure we survived until the cash arrived. Each day was a roller coaster ride full of equal parts panic and adrenaline, exhilaration and relief. We proved to ourselves over and over again that we were so much more capable than we thought, able to seize opportunities much bigger than our perceived capacity to deliver.

I was relieved when Bob relayed the news that our request for a two-week postponement had been accepted. The two-week grace period would give me the chance to make sure our affairs were in order. I assumed the audit would be a fairly straightforward process, pulling together the relevant paperwork and making sure it was ready to submit to the auditors. I was prepared for it to be tedious, even exhausting, but I was sure we'd be fine.

I planned to spend some extra time in the office in the evenings to look for the potential problem areas on their radar. I wasn't prepared at all for what I found . . . or rather, for what I didn't find.

Within a couple of hours of digging, I discovered that certain important records were missing. Not only that, I realized we didn't have all of the necessary insurance policies and bonds required for us to operate lawfully. As with any startup, we had some holes that needed filling. We had some processes that had fallen through the cracks and weren't in place. In just my first pass through our paperwork, it was evident that we had enough deficiencies to fail our audit.

THE TRIPLE THREAT

We were in trouble. I felt completely out of my element. My confidence was rocked.

In the next thirty minutes, I progressed through three distinct stages of thinking. Since that time, I've learned how common these stages are. When not addressed, these stages form a "triple threat" to progress.

DENIAL

The first stage I entered was Denial. This is fairly common when anyone encounters something tragic like a job loss or death. I wanted to believe my company was in good shape, ready and able to weather any storm. Maybe the auditors just called us by mistake. This audit couldn't have been meant for us. Certainly this wasn't our year for an audit.

As soon as the thought entered my mind, I discounted it. I knew that, as an insurance company, by law we were to be audited every three to five years. This audit was real and not the result of some clerical mistake. I was just going to have to deal with it.

MAKING EXCUSES

After climbing out of the mire of Denial, I got hit with a wave of Excuses as to why this was happening. Okay, I told myself, we're being audited. Everyone gets audited. But we're a good company, dedicated to doing things the right way.

I shook myself out of my funk and readdressed the situation. I dug deeper into the paperwork.

In this last three-year period, we had faced significant and costly challenges, including a strategic partner who went out of business, an attempted hostile takeover by a competitor, regulatory and funding issues, and more.

The period had taken its toll on me personally as well. I had to navigate through the troubled waters of issues associated with a failed business partnership. And if that weren't enough, I had been diagnosed and treated for breast cancer. Not only was each day a fight to keep the business alive, but each day was literally a life versus death battle to survive cancer, multiple surgeries, and infections. Not to mention the recovery process itself. I felt threatened on every front, professional, legal, emotional, and physical. Circumstances outside our control blew up like landmines with every step we took.

Making our situation even tougher was the fact that our industry was rapidly changing and being redefined by the federal government. My company, though small, was facing the same regulatory requirements of the larger multibillion-dollar companies. The problem was that we didn't have the deep pockets the bigger companies did. There was no way we could afford to monitor or influence all the legislative decisions that would directly impact us.

We had a long list of legitimate excuses for being out of compliance. I could show this list to any of my friends, family, or co-workers, and they would immediately think the same thing I was thinking: It's no wonder we're out of compliance! Look at all we've had to deal with.

ASSIGNING BLAME

But after slogging through Denial, then making Excuses, I arrived at the third stage. I began to point fingers and assign Blame. We all do that from time to time, don't we? If something bad has happened, someone must be to blame. I ran down the roster of all the usual suspects, trying to pick out the guiltiest parties. I thought about my competitors, I thought about the auditors themselves. Finally, after wrestling with these crazy theories for several minutes, I shook my head. What was I thinking?

It was in this moment, at my desk, that I experienced a life-changing epiphany. I realized that Denial, Excuses, and Blame accomplish nothing in an audit. My feelings would hold absolutely no sway in the audit process. The audit is simply a cold-hard snapshot at whether you're compliant with the law or not.

Not only does the "triple threat" accomplish nothing, they are the great time robbers in both business and life. The amount of time and energy we spend dealing with these three thieves should be directed toward the main objective, which in my case was a routine audit. Denial, Excuses, and Blame only distract us from moving forward.

A KEY THOUGHT

This was such a simple concept, but it changed my whole view of life and business. I finally understood that it all boils down to this key thought: *If you want to be successful, you have to be in compliance with the laws of what it takes to be successful in that area.*

The purpose of any audit is simply to verify that we are in compliance with the law. Whether it is the law of the land, a law of physics, a law of success, or the law of unintended consequences, either we are in compliance or we're not. If we are not in compliance, then we are destined to fail.

Let me give you an example. If you want to lose weight, you're going to have to act in compliance with the laws of losing weight. Makes perfect sense, right? If you want to drop those unwanted pounds, you're going to have to follow an effective and appropriate strategy like burning more calories than you're taking in. It does no good to deny this fact. Excuses aren't relevant and no one else is to blame. At some point, you're going to have to own the process and figure out a way to burn more calories than you're taking in.

This principle is even more powerful when a sense of urgency is added. Once there is a deadline in place, the project or goal can no longer stretch out to infinity. You can talk all about how nice it would be to have a high school reunion, or you can talk in broad general terms about plans for the wedding of one of your kids, but once a date is set, you quickly move beyond the theoretical and into the real. It's no longer time for dreaming; it's time for taking action.

It may not sound like much of a realization to you now.

But that evening, sitting at my desk, the realization hit me like a bolt of lightning.

It was then that I experienced what would become a life-changing revelation, and I use the term "revelation" on purpose. Revelation is a spiritual term, and that's what this truth was to me. This revelation would revolutionize my business and influence my life's path. Not only that, I knew that the steps we took in our audit, anyone could take in order to achieve success. The audit as a road map to success began to take shape in my mind. The AUDIT Principle would have global application, reaching far beyond my own small business.

WE PASSED!

Ultimately we were able to identify where we were out of compliance. We worked night and day to fix our problems and get back into shape. We were ready when the auditor showed up at our door, and we passed with flying colors.

That first audit changed my life and launched our company up to a new level of success we had never before achieved. We were diligent to put systems in place as well as identify and improve our processes. Through the experience of grinding through that first audit, we had gained the confidence of the auditing agency. Even more beneficial to me was gaining confidence in my organization and my ability to lead them.

That audit was a turning point for me because of the struggles I had with my own self-confidence as an executive. I hadn't gone to business school; I hadn't even taken an accounting class. In fact, in school my weakest subjects were math and science.

And yet here I was, the founder and CEO of a highly regulated financial institution called an insurance company. We contracted with thousands of health care providers, paid claims for thousands of members, processed millions of dollars in premiums and claims, and designed and managed our own IT systems and processes.

As tough as that audit was, it validated to the world that we were a great company, full of highly skilled and well-managed people. That audit showed that I was qualified as a business leader. That feeling alone made the whole process worth it.

Over time my one little company grew into four companies and eventually expanded into multiple states. The once stressful and harrowing audit process became routine for us. And while every audit was costly, each one proved to be valuable, taking our organization to an even higher level of productivity and excellence.

THE **AUDIT** PRINCIPLE

This book will show you how the AUDIT Principle can transform your life. It's a key to success, whether in business, marriage, raising children, losing weight, or any other area of life.

The AUDIT Principle isn't just relegated to the areas of business or taxes either. It's a universal law, true in every situation. It's a principle that, when applied, will not only perpetuate personal success but also assist in helping others fulfill their own goals, dreams, and visions. By understanding the power of the AUDIT Principle and applying its five simple steps, there is absolutely no area in a person's life or business where success cannot be achieved.

Don't be fooled. Just because the AUDIT Principle is simple doesn't mean it's easy. But if you desire to do better in your job, your health, your productivity, or your happiness, and you're willing to work through the process, the value of following these steps far outweighs the cost and effort.

Too often people fail to even try to go after their goals and dreams because they believe the myths that they are too young or too old, they don't have the money or connections, or they don't have the experience or the right credentials.

The great news is that your success isn't based on any of these myths. That's all they are—myths. Success for any venture comes when you assess where you are, then understand your target and where you want to go. Next you decide what vehicle is required to get to your destination, imagine your plan to get there, and muster the determination to see it through all the way to the end.

When you conduct your own internal audits along the way, you are able to determine if your strategies and actions are in compliance with the laws of success that relate to what you're trying to achieve. Get rid of the Denial, throw away the Excuses and the Blame that only trip you up and stop your momentum. If conditions change, don't blame the market; use what you learn from your audit to get in compliance with the new conditions! If something isn't working, give yourself an audit to determine the changes that need to be made.

IF OTHERS CAN DO IT, YOU CAN DO IT TOO!

An important step on the road to success is to allow yourself to be encouraged by the successes of others. "If others can do it, YOU can do it too."

I was a widowed single mom. I quit my job at the age of thirty-nine without the benefit of a business degree. Not only that, I had very little in the way of financial resources. And yet I was able to start a company from scratch and sell it to a multi billion-dollar company. Then I was asked to stay on and serve as their CEO. That story still amazes me. If I could do all that, given the limitations and obstacles I had to wrestle with, imagine what you can accomplish!

Raising necessary capital, navigating complicated regulatory and IT requirements, and just remaining competitive day after day were all daunting tasks for me. I had a load of limitations but was able to succeed in spite of them.

Maybe your dream isn't to start an insurance company. But if you have dreams of your own, rest assured, they are worth pursuing, even though those dreams might seem impossible to you today. Yes, it will be tough. Yes, you will encounter resistance. But the reward is worth it. You can succeed!

DEFINING MOMENTS

S INCE I FIRST BEGAN SHARING the AUDIT Principle with others, many have asked how the principle became real to me. Obviously, as I wrote in the first chapter, that first audit had a lot to do with the principle taking shape in my mind in a form I could share with others. But when I look back over my life, I can clearly see that the seeds of the AUDIT Principle were being planted at critical moments all throughout my life.

All of us encounter times when we're ready to learn new things, times when we're more open to counsel and advice, or times when difficult circumstances cause us to dig deeper to find out what we're made of. We all go through times that affect us deeply; these experiences seem divine, as if God Himself is trying to show us something about ourselves. It's how we respond in these critical moments that defines the kind of person we're destined to become. I call these times "Defining Moments."

We all have a measure of greatness residing deep within

us. That greatness is unlikely to emerge without the defining moments to draw it out. It's like the woman who finds the supernatural strength to lift a car off her baby after an accident. The strength was always there . . . she just didn't know it until she needed it. In her case, the real defining moment wasn't so much the accident but the strength she found because of it.

Defining moments sometimes don't seem like much at the time they're happening. They're just experiences that are difficult or troubling. Sometimes they only emerge years later when we look at them in the context of the present.

But there are other times when we have the feeling, even at the time it's happening, that this moment will somehow define the person we are to become. Many of my defining moments affected me in exactly that way.

DASHED EXPECTATIONS

"Jane Ann, I see you floating down a river without a rudder or sail. I am really worried about you."

Those words hit me like a ton of bricks. I thought I was on the right track, heading in the right direction. To think that a teacher I looked up to so highly thought this of me was devastating.

It was my senior year of high school. I had enrolled in a unique and popular class taught by two very passionate, dedicated and nontraditional teachers, teachers I admired. These two teachers had joined together with the objective of reaching kids using real life application techniques versus the more traditional academic-style of teaching.

I remember them assigning only one homework project during that entire semester. The assignment was to keep a daily journal. We were instructed to write every day. We were to write about what we were learning, experiencing, and feeling. We had to turn in our assignments to the teachers a couple of weeks before the summer break. Then on the last day of school, they would give our journals back along with their personal written feedback and advice.

Over the next several months, I diligently worked on that project and wrote down my thoughts every single day. Because of the "coolness factor" of one particular teacher, I was exceptionally open and honest as I wrote about my life experiences and emotions. I imagined her reading my journal and writing a very personal message about how enlightened and self-aware I was. Surely she would write about my mature spirituality and intellectualism in her comments back to me.

On the due date, we dutifully turned in our assignments and waited for the last day of class when the teachers would hand them back to us along with their comments. My expectations were running high. I was convinced that she would applaud me for not only possessing profound and critical thinking skills, but also for my courage and passion in experiencing my young life to the fullest.

At last the big day arrived, and the teachers handed back our assignments. I couldn't wait to read mine. I eagerly opened my journal and saw her handwritten note across the front page. She had written, *Jane Ann, I see you floating down a river without a rudder or sail. I am really worried about you.*

She wrote a bit more, but those are the words I remember.

Those are the words that rocked the foundation of my young world. It was a simple illustration, and one I understood perfectly. I had grown up sailing and I understood the analogy. She was saying that I was broken, that I was merely floating around, carried by the waves, with no direction or sense of purpose. I was living life aimlessly.

Needless to say, this wasn't what I imagined at all. She was not enthusiastic about what I'd written. She wasn't enthralled with my intellect, charm, or life experience. She wasn't even encouraging. I was beyond disappointed and deflated. I was devastated. Her insightful comments and how I ultimately responded to them would become perhaps the most profound defining moment in my life up to that point.

Defining moments are interesting things. The dictionary defines a "defining moment" as a point at which one's essential nature or character reveals itself. I see now that what the teacher wrote to me was integral to me becoming the woman I am today. Though I've wandered from time to time, I've always longed to find my purpose and direction. The last thing I would want to be said about me is that I was like a ship without a rudder, with an undetermined direction or purpose.

MY VERY FIRST BUSINESS PLAN

As long as I can remember, I knew I wanted to live a life of significance. I didn't just want to live my life for me. I wanted to make a difference in the world.

Driven by that sense of purpose, I raced home as soon as school was over. I ran upstairs to the privacy of my room and grabbed a notepad with the goal of reinventing myself. My days of drifting aimlessly were over. I was determined right then and there to decide what I would become in life and develop a plan so I could see it through. In my own simplistic and naïve way, that afternoon, and into the evening, I drafted the bare bones of what would become my very first business plan.

Without any direction or coaching from anyone, I began to write, making a list with two columns. The first column was titled, "What's important to me." This column consisted of everything I thought my future career path would need to have:

- A job where I could be my own boss

- A job based on a skill that would be in demand in case of war, depression, drought, famine, or any other disaster

- A job that included some element of art to take advantage of my artistic abilities

- A job that would build wealth

- A job that would allow me to make a difference with my life

Then, in the second column I listed the kinds of jobs that would meet each of my criteria. But as I reviewed the requirements listed in the first column, there seemed to be only one job that covered all my criteria. It appeared to me that I needed to become a doctor, possibly a surgeon. My reasoning was simple:

- *Most doctors own their own practice and are their own boss*

- *Most doctors make a lot of money*

- *Surgery requires artistic talent*

- *Doctors are always needed, especially during times of war and economic hardship*

- *Doctors heal diseases; therefore they make a difference in the lives of others*

I had done it! In a very logical and analytical, non-emotional way, I had arrived at what would become the new vehicle to my purpose in life. A doctor! I ran down the stairs, waving the list over my head. I shouted, "Mom and Dad! I've decided what I'm going to do with my life! I'm going to become a doctor!"

As I think back to that experience, the defining moment of the teacher's words that led me home to make a plan to become a doctor, I'm still astonished. That whole exercise probably only took a couple of hours and that plan was so flawed in many ways, but the process was invaluable and paved the way for who I am today.

In the end, I didn't become a doctor at all. It didn't take long for me to accept the fact that I didn't enjoy science or medicine. I'd learned to get As, but it was a struggle and wasn't something I wanted to spend the rest of my life working at. When life got hard, my passion for becoming a doctor wasn't powerful enough to persevere, pay the price, and see the process through.

However, it was in following my plan to get into medical school that I discovered that I enjoyed and was good at politics, business, and a whole different skillset.

Anytime we have a goal, dream, or vision and pursue it with a sound plan, we will find that as we walk it out, we will be presented with unexpected opportunities. This allows us access to unanticipated influence. If we have the courage to pass through those unexpected doors, seize unanticipated opportunities, and build upon new relationships, we will always end up with a bigger vision or outcome. As a result, our world, resources, skills, and relationships expand beyond our dreams.

The principles I learned through the process of eliminating medicine as a consideration for a lifelong career are a critical ingredient to my success today. Our lives are often defined by several key moments. I never dreamed I would be an insurance executive. I never would have written that into any plan.

FINDING PURPOSE

A defining moment that led to the writing of this book came in response to suddenly finding myself a widow, a single mom, and the sole provider for my two-year-old son. In the midst of tragedy, grief, and exhaustion, I discovered a deeper sense of purpose, clarity, and urgency rising up within me.

This new sense of purpose led me to expand my mission. First and foremost, I wanted to provide the best life possible for my son. I wanted to live a life full of meaning and at the same time, I wanted to support, help, and inspire others by going to places where few were willing to go and touch the people others weren't touching.

But with the strong sense of purpose and mission also came a strong sense of self-doubt. Would this clarity give me the courage I needed to rise up and face the challenges, or would I shrink back and fail to push through?

ENDURING CHALLENGES

Challenges come in all shapes and sizes, but they all have one thing in common. By definition, challenges are . . . challenging. The death of a loved one is one of the most difficult challenges we all must face.

After an eight-month battle of fighting off an aggressive and relentless attack of lung and bone cancer, my husband David was rushed to the hospital, where he fell into a coma. He passed from life to death only seven days into his one and only hospital stay.

Over that period of time, I pleaded with him more than once, "David, use your faith! We need to fight this thing. We can do it."

I was so scared! I remember telling him in those difficult months that there was no way I could make it by myself. I knew I would be unable to manage being a single mom.

I didn't fully grasp the depth of the physical pain he was experiencing. I didn't understand the magnitude of the battle he was facing. All I knew was that he was my rock, my protector, my best friend and lover, and the father of my son. I couldn't imagine surviving life without him. I couldn't see a future unless he was there by my side.

It was in those scary moments that David would talk to me. His words haunt me to this day. When I was most frightened, he would encourage me by telling me, "Jane Ann, you'll be fine without me. In fact, you will soar! You'll succeed in whatever you put your hand to."

That was David's way of telling me he knew he wasn't going to win this battle. Even in his pain, he wasn't thinking of himself. He wanted me to know that in spite of my fears of being a single mom, I would do great.

I endured the vigil beside my husband in that lonely, depressing hospital room throughout the entire coma, all seven days. I was scared that if I left, even for a moment, he wouldn't be there when I returned. Other than a quick shower or a meal, the only time I left was when I ventured downstairs to the little chapel.

I was fortunate to be at his bedside when David's eyes opened just briefly. He turned his head and took one last glance at me, then closed his eyes for the last time. Over the next few hours the monitors began to beep and chirp as the numbers displaying on the various machines began to drop. A short time later, he was gone. Just like that, my vigil was over. I had lost my husband.

That was the most painful and challenging night I had ever experienced. I just stood by my husband's bed praying silently. I didn't know what else to do. Once again, Denial crept into my thoughts. I prayed the monitors were wrong and David would suddenly wake up. Through the fog of my grief, I prayed for a miracle.

During those seven days in the hospital, my pastor and his wife always seemed to show up at just the right time. They were there the night David died. After a short time, my pastor took me by the hand and quietly said, "Jane Ann, David is gone."

Tenderly, he took me in his arms and began to weep. It was his tears and his sorrow that allowed me to give way to my own grief. In the warmth and safety of my pastor's embrace, I let go and cried.

Forever etched into my memory will be the moment when it was time to say good-bye. I can't explain how hard it was to walk out of the hospital room after David's death. I remember standing by David's bed and gazing out the door that led to the nurse's counter. I knew that for me to leave that room meant crossing a kind of line in the sand. Once I crossed the threshold of that doorway, there was no coming back. I was not only letting go of my husband, I was letting go of the only life I knew, forever.

I would be walking into an unknown future. I would leave behind all the dreams, visions, and goals that, only a few hours before, I shared with my precious husband. Defining moments can look pretty daunting before you pass through them. Saying good-bye to David and stepping across that threshold was a moment that defined the person I am.

My pastor and his wife walked me through the dark parking lot to my car. As we passed under a lamppost, my pastor stopped me and took me by the shoulders. He locked eyes with me and repeated what he'd said in the hospital room. "Jane Ann, David is gone." But then he added, "But your goals, dreams, and visions aren't. Don't ever let go of them."

Those were the perfect words at the perfect time. They didn't just encourage me in that moment; they gave me a sense of hope for the future.

David was generous and kind. He loved people dearly. He was purpose-driven and taught me more in our almost six years of marriage than I could ever attempt to include in this book. The one thing I can say with absolute confidence is that he was right. The words that scared me so much at the time were true. I would be able to move on with life and do great.

THE VEHICLE PRINCIPLE:

When I started the company, the first thing I did was to write a business plan. A written plan is the place to articulate all those dreams that have been rattling around in your head. On paper, the dreams begin to take shape in a form that can be communicated more easily to others. Certain aspects of the dream will fall away while others crystallize in a whole new light.

While working through my business plan, I experienced another defining moment. This was an "Aha!" moment, as I suddenly understood the power behind my decision to start a company. In that moment I caught hold of a principle, which I now call the Vehicle Principle. This principle led to me writing a personal mission statement that became my guiding light over the years to come.

I will build a company and sell it for millions of dollars. It will be a vehicle that supports my personal goals, dreams, and visions, and it will support the goals, dreams, and visions of the partners, employees, shareholders, and clients who are connected with us.

Since those days, I have presented this principle as a core value to each employee and client that I advise. I tell them,

"Your company, career, or decision should be a vehicle that supports you in achieving your own goals, dreams, and visions." With this understanding, they can measure whether or not the job, investment, or decision is right for them.

This valuable principle has the potential to guide people, keeping their career in proper perspective. I've found through the years that applying this principle can help with any decision, from a significant purchase to getting married to making an investment. "Will this vehicle get me where I want to go?"

This Vehicle Principle can help the employee, business owner, manager, or organization design a personal mission statement of their own that will measure their strategies and career choices with the end in mind. This is the most fundamental key to success. Because in identifying the target before getting started, we set into motion the decision to live and act intentionally while measuring our resources and time.

This principle became a beacon in determining what life path I would take as a widow and single mom. It has continued to guide me in many life decisions over the years and has become a key component of the AUDIT Principle. Time and time again the application of the Vehicle Principle has caused me to ask the right questions and follow up with proper goals and strategies.

It was this line of thinking that led me to distill all the uncertainties, all the unknowns, and all the worries down to this simple question: "What vehicle exists that will allow me to pursue my goals, dreams, and visions?" Or to put a finer point on it, "What vehicle will help me to achieve my goals, dreams, and visions *in the shortest amount of time?*"

This defining moment led me to wrestle with the answers to this question. It required me to take a step back and look at my life objectively, strategically, and even tactically.

MARKERS ALONG THE WAY

Along the many hiking trails in my adopted home state of Utah, you'll see stacks of stones. These stacks are usually just a foot or two tall, but they have a very important purpose. In the wilderness, there are no nice detailed signs showing you which way to go. Rather, there are stacks of stones called "cairns." Cairns are placed in critical, strategic places along the trail to clearly mark the path you're supposed to follow.

In your life, your defining moments are a lot like those cairns along the hiking trail, pointing you in the right direction.

Whether it was as a senior in high school letting a teacher's hard words push me toward defining the kind of person I wanted to be or the difficult moment in a small hospital room or the emergence of a whole new personal mission statement, these defining moments led me in the right direction along my path.

I have no doubt that you've been able to identify some defining moments in your own life as well. Once you're able to identify these significant moments, take some time to ponder them carefully. You will see themes or similarities emerge. These moments will point you in a specific direction, encouraging you along your future path. Like my situation, your defining moments will serve as signposts along your life's journey.

THE BIRTH OF
THE AUDIT PRINCIPLE

EVER SINCE the AUDIT Principle revealed itself to me, I've been able to see its roots throughout many chapters of my life. Today I can see this life-changing principle has been foundational to each success I've experienced.

The chapters before mentioned defining moments, relationships, situations, and circumstances that have led me to where I am today. The same is true of you. Your life is a result of the decisions you've made and relationships you've formed along your life's journey. If you're not satisfied with the results you see in your life, you can change that negative trajectory by applying the AUDIT Principle outlined in this book.

To help you understand the AUDIT Principle, it's important to give you some context, to tell you a little more about myself. Newton's Third Law states that for every action, there is an equal and opposite reaction. If we don't like the results, we must change the actions that are causing them. It's true in science and it's true in life.

BEGIN WITH THE END IN MIND

My parents were always "big picture" thinkers. And the way they thought couldn't help but influence the way I learned to think from the time I was very young. Like them, I've always been more successful solving a problem or challenge by looking at the end from the beginning. If you want to end up in a certain place, you must first consider where you're starting.

I grew up in Southern California. My mom and dad were careful planners and believed that a strategy put in place early on would produce the desired results. A great example of this is how we ended up in California in the first place. While many people don't even consider where they are living as a negotiable item, my parents thought otherwise. They actually did the research, studying several locations around the country and ultimately deciding that California would be the best place for us to live.

They wanted to be able to take advantage of the opportunities available to those who lived in California. They studied the demographics, the school systems; they even studied the weather patterns along the entire coast of California before determining that Newport Beach was the place they wanted to live. In their view, Newport Beach held the greatest promise for their young family. Always with an eye to the future, they bought property that would generate the greatest return on investment while at the same time providing us children the greatest chances for success. My dad was a forward thinker to say the least.

I didn't grow up wealthy. My dad wasn't in finance and didn't own his own shipping company. He was an orthodontist, and we certainly weren't rich, especially by Newport Beach standards. But while my dad made a decent income with his profession, he made much of his money with a handful of wise real estate investments. He had the ability to look into the future and position himself to be in the right place at the right time. His ability to see the end from the beginning is one of the traits he passed down to me and is one of the key components in the AUDIT Principle. Even though death isn't a pleasant topic to think about, my parents were diligent to have detailed trusts in place, including designated guardians for me and my siblings, along with other support systems that would automatically kick in if my mom and dad both died at the same time. My parents wanted to make sure we were provided for. They thought of everything, to the extent of even flying in separate airplanes when vacationing so if one plane went down, the other parent would survive to raise us.

In addition to having a detailed will and trust, my father confided in me that he had hidden a check for several thousand dollars. If anything were to happen to him and my mom, he instructed me to immediately cash the check so we would have money to live on until their estate could be distributed.

The day after my dad died, I remembered the check. My mom immediately cashed it, and that money provided the necessary funds for us to live on until the bank and courts could settle my dad's estate. What a great life lesson from my father. He always looked ahead.

Believing the bank would bring an additional level of investment expertise to support my mom, my dad selected the bank to be the co-executor of their estate. That way the bank would control half of our family's estate and my mom would control the other half. But ironically, through a series of bad investments, the bank lost almost their entire portion of our estate. However, my mom was able to invest what was left on her side to rebuild the estate to where it once had been. Even now, well into her nineties, my mom continues to manage her investments on her own, always thinking ahead. Thinking ahead is a principle that's been lived out in front of me my whole life.

My parents were amazing, adventuresome, generous, and compassionate. They were incredibly committed to my siblings and me. My success is due in large part to their commitment and the generosity of their time and resources. My parents are the ones who gave me the mindset to succeed. I owe them a debt I can never repay.

A SIGN OF THINGS TO COME

Since I was a young girl, there's been an awareness that I was created for a greater purpose, that there was a plan in place, something bigger that I was a part of.

I still remember the first time this thought occurred to me. Oddly enough, it all started with a trip to the dentist's office. Isn't it funny how some of the most positive moments in our life begin as negative ones? This was one of the few times I was punished and grounded as a child. But out of that punishment came a very clear picture of what my life was going to be about.

My dad had taken me to a dentist friend of his for a routine visit. For a child, a routine dental visit can be a scary thing. Bright lights, strange instruments, weird sounds, and to top it off, a stranger sticks his fingers in your mouth! I was unsettled, to say the least! During the examination, I must have panicked, and when the dentist put his thumb in my mouth, I bit down as hard as I could. No matter what the adults in the room were doing to get me to let up, I wouldn't release this poor man's thumb!

The dentist was in shock and pain, and my father was frustrated and angry. The higher the stress level in the room rose, the harder I bit down. Finally (and uncharacteristically of my dad), he gave in. He decided to negotiate a compromise.

He promised to take me home if, and only if, I would let go of the dentist's thumb. But the agreement bit both ways. I had to understand that while the rest of the kids at home would be enjoying the beautiful summer day in the backyard swimming pool, I would be relegated to my bedroom. I agreed and let go of that poor man's thumb. We left the office and sulked back to the car for the trip home.

Later that afternoon as I lay on my bed crying, surrounded by stuffed animals and listening to the laughter of the other kids in the backyard pool, I experienced a powerful sense of Presence.

I can't honestly say I heard a tangible voice. It was more like a thought or message I received with my inner ear, perhaps with my heart. The gist of the message was that there was so much more to life than I had the capability to understand at that moment. Somehow, down deep inside, I knew that there would come a time when I would go to places where few people were willing to go and have the opportunity to touch lives that many people would never experience.

That message remained with me. It forms the very cornerstone of my personal mission statement. It sticks with me as a core guiding principle that's just as real to me today as it was on that beautiful summer day so many years ago.

MY SPIRITUAL BEGINNINGS

From a young girl I was raised in the Lutheran church, but it was a Presbyterian youth camp during the summer of my sixth-grade year in school that officially started my life's spiritual journey.

I was young and passionate, and I embraced my newly found faith with a zeal that, frankly, concerned my parents. They were afraid that I might be obsessed with Christianity and somehow go off the deep end. They believed in God and the value of going to church, but the hunger I had to follow God concerned them.

At this time there was an unusual movement emerging. This movement was called the Jesus Movement, and it started in Southern California where our family lived. Eventually it spread across the world. Members of the movement were called Jesus People or Jesus Freaks. Unlike many other spiritual movements and revivals, this one had no single leader, no one voice. Although I was too young to be a part of it, the movement captured my attention and my desire to understand spiritual things. I had a front row seat and watched as this movement went mainstream.

I was drawn by the dynamic preaching, as well as the contemporary music common to their services. There were church-sponsored concerts that I found it hard to stay away from. The church would regularly organize huge baptism services down at Corona del Mar beach. It was an amazing phenomenon to watch the hippies find God and seemingly walk away from their drug addiction.

I attended every service and concert that I was able to catch a ride to. At most of their services, one or more of the kids would get up and share their stories, which were usually dramatic and tended to follow the same progression. First, they'd been serious drug users. Second, they'd experienced a dramatic encounter with God. And third, they'd walked away from their drug use.

They shared how God had set them free from addiction, which led them to having a personal relationship with Him. They shared about how they talked to God and God talked back. Every story caused me to hunger for a similar relationship with God. But no matter how much I prayed and read my Bible, I couldn't seem to find a relationship with God like these kids had.

It was one night after listening to one of these dramatic testimonies that I came up with an idea that I thought would allow me to finally find a relationship with God like the one these kids talked about. In my immaturity, I figured that the first step was to start where they started. I decided to become a drug addict, that way God could set me free from drugs just like He did for them. Then maybe I would have an encounter with God like the one they talked about.

Before that night was over I had taken the first steps of my new quest toward drug addiction. I made a call from the church to a friend of a friend and bought my first drugs on the way home. Within just a few months, I was taking enough "speed" (methamphetamine) that I had developed a stutter when I spoke. By the end of my freshman year of high school, I was taking large amounts of LSD. There were few days during those years when I wasn't high. The high school years, which for many students are their happiest, are all a blur to me because of my dependence on drugs.

Throughout those years my hunger for spiritual things never waned, and I routinely reached out to my youth pastors and other friends from church. But over time, my church friends decided I was much too flaky. My drug use caused my behavior to be erratic, and as a result, they wanted less and less to do with me. The more they turned their backs on me, the less I cared about them or their spiritual influence on my life. Consequently, the more drugs I did, the more my spiritual quest shifted from a hunger for the God of my youth to a keen interest in Eastern religions, mysticism, and metaphysics.

FINDING CONSCIOUSNESS

The shift completed one night at a party with several of my friends. I took some acid (LSD) with others, and in the midst of our conversation, we began questioning the meaning behind the word "it." We were totally absorbed in this quest for truth. The next thing I knew (although my memory is understandably a little hazy), our conversation morphed into what we believed was an out-of-body experience that lasted several hours. Together we believed we had transcended time and space and become one with consciousness. We had discovered the ultimate definition of what "it" means: "All is all, and that is all, and that is it." Brilliant!

That night I was awestruck. In the midst of my mental fog, I was convinced that my Christian blinders had fallen away and I had experienced what Eastern religious culture calls "Enlightenment."

A couple of us continued to pursue experiences like that. We wanted to replicate what we'd shared. It was in a search for explanations that we discovered there were scientists and teachers from Harvard taking acid and having similar experiences and then writing about them. Dr. Richard Albert and Timothy Leary were among the leaders of this movement.

Suddenly we had validation that our experiences were legitimate, that our spiritual quest was real. For the remainder of my high school and college years, I studied meditation through an organization called Self-Realization Fellowship. I became immersed in other Eastern teachings as well.

The ironic thing is that while I was seeking complete freedom through consciousness, my life had never felt so empty. I had come to a place where there were no absolutes. My friends who were physics students supported these Eastern concepts with explanations that we were simply molecules moving at different rates of speed and frequencies. Eastern religion taught that our physical life was only an illusion, what they referred to as "Maya."

It was in this context that I shared some of these experiences in my high school journal for a class my senior year. Now you can understand the concern of my teacher when she wrote that she saw me as a sailboat just floating down the river with no destination. It was her comments after reading my journal that caused me to temporarily "reset" my life and map out a whole new plan.

KARATE'S INFLUENCE

A significant influence that helped me transition into my new life in college was my love of martial arts and the pursuit of my black belt. Of course, this was also consistent with the influence of Eastern thought. As a result, I became very disciplined and ambitious in working out and in life in general.

From the time I was a young girl, I loved the martial arts and dreamed of earning my black belt. I watched the Green Hornet on TV and never missed an episode of Kung Fu. When Bruce Lee movies came to town, I was first in line at the theater.

When karate studios began to pop up around town, I pleaded with my parents to enroll me. In all those years, karate was the only sport I can remember where my parents turned me down. My mom was scared that if I learned karate, I might actually use it on someone and get hurt.

Despite my relentless pleas, compelling arguments, and growing passion, my parents stayed firm in their stance against karate. The problem was that the more they said no, the more passionate about the pursuit I became. Where most adolescent girls had posters of teenage heart-throbs, my walls were adorned with pictures of Bruce Lee, Chuck Norris, and other popular martial artists. While my peers subscribed to magazines like *Equestrian* and *Teen Beat*, I subscribed to *Black Belt*.

This passion intensified within me throughout high school,

ironically keeping pace with my drug use. When I turned eighteen, one of the first things I did was enroll in the local Kenpo Karate School. Now that I was of legal age, I no longer needed my parents' consent.

As a brand-new college freshman, I found that it was karate that taught me discipline and focus, two skills I neglected to develop in high school. Karate brought focus to my life and helped counter the negative effects resulting from my continued drug abuse. Most karate schools teach by creating imaginary situations and then teaching students how to get out of them. In other words, karate provides a plan for when bad things might happen. This kind of planning and forward thinking really helped me focus. With the help of karate, I progressed from a failing student, barely graduating from high school, to a stellar college student.

Karate is the practical application of Newton's Laws of Motion. It's a series of moves or techniques that when followed appropriately allow you to use your opponent's motion and body mass to your advantage. It's a great life lesson, teaching that if the technique doesn't work, you're going to have to make an adjustment. It was karate that began to shape the concept in my mind of aligning my actions with correct laws.

More than simply learning how to break boards or flip a big man to the ground, I learned to step into an attack. Like a firefighter running into danger, the answer is often not backing away but rushing toward the battle.

A REAL-LIFE TEST

This actually happened to me one time when I entered a public restroom. Once inside, a large man lunged at me. Without even thinking, I stepped into his lunge, hooked the wrist of his extended arm, and snapped his elbow. Then I ran.

What fascinated me most about this experience was that the technique I used wasn't an advanced karate technique at all. In fact, it was a "yellow belt" move, one of the earliest and easiest moves I'd been taught. When the man lunged at me, I didn't hesitate because I had practiced this move in every class since I had begun taking karate lessons. The technique of moving into the attacker, hooking his wrist, and snapping his elbow had become instinctive.

Three dynamics made the difference that day. The first is that I kept things simple. The technique was a single fluid move. This was a move I had practiced almost every day for years. Like most schools, learning was based on a lot of repetition, and we started every class reviewing beginner techniques. This allowed us to build a strong foundation of basic moves; the most advanced techniques were built upon earlier, beginner techniques.

The second dynamic is practice. I had practiced that move every day, so I had developed the critical skill and muscle memory needed to be successful. When attacked, I responded instinctively.

The third dynamic is strategy. Most of the time, we don't respond with a strategy, we just react. And often it's the reaction that causes us problems moving forward. In this case, I had a plan in mind of what I would do if I were ever attacked. Had I reacted to his lunge by stepping back, I would have been caught against the door. By stepping into the attack, I quickly gained control of the situation and was able to snap his elbow.

The key to my success that day was that I had developed the mindset and I had a strategy, a plan of what to do if I were attacked, and I practiced my plan over and over. I committed it to instinct. Then, when the attack came, I was prepared and stepped into it, executing the plan.

This principle can apply in every area of your life. It's not about how smart, big, wealthy, or educated you are. Rather it's about mindset, strategy, and practice. In fact, often times, the bigger the attacker, the easier the take-down.

My experience with karate also helped me to understand the significance of goal setting and how accomplishing goals is easier when the process is broken down into smaller steps. I had the goal to earn a black belt. But I couldn't earn a black belt without first earning a yellow, orange, purple, blue, green, and different degrees of brown and red belts.

No matter how athletic or how agile, everyone has to start at the beginning as a white belt. Like every karate student, I dreamed of the end from the beginning. The goal and the dream of earning the black belt kept me going throughout all the incremental steps.

The most valuable lesson was the understanding and practical application that I could do what others believed impossible. Where hardship might discourage others, it only strengthened my resolve. Karate taught me the valuable lesson that if I followed certain principles and laws, it didn't matter what other people said or thought; I could overcome any limitation.

While in college I continued to train in karate and study metaphysical and Eastern philosophy but without the influence of LSD. I was still a drug user; I continued to use cocaine and pot socially and recreationally. This wasn't odd behavior for a college student in those days. Doing drugs was affecting me in a very negative way, but it was couched as such a positive thing to do. I was surrounded by this kind of behavior; my friends, who were also successful, were doing the same thing; even some of my teachers were involved. As a young student, I thought it was fun, and I was flattered to be accepted into their circle.

But my life had become an intense struggle between good and bad, light and dark. On the one hand I was excelling in school and rubbing shoulders with all the right people, making friends and building my network of connections. To the outward observer, I was ambitious and excelling. I had taken a debate class with the goal of building skill and confidence in public speaking. I ran for student office and was elected. Then, during my second year, I became the college's first female student body president, which caught the attention of the local Republican Party.

Soon I was serving as a student ambassador at prestigious political events that included photo ops with politicians, celebrities, and rock stars. I was invited to important fundraisers and even landed an opportunity to travel across the country with President Ronald Reagan's campaign. I was moving in the fast lane, participating in the early environmental movement with Buckminster Fuller and his team of students. On many levels, I was on the right track, ambitious, focused, and successful. As a result of my high-profile involvement in student government and local community politics, I built an impressive resume while developing important relationships with people of influence.

But my life was a juggling act. I was still taking drugs and seeking the relief and the high they provided me. Somewhere in my consciousness, I realized my lifestyle wasn't sustainable, but I didn't know how to stop.

TRAGEDY STRIKES

Then suddenly and unexpectedly, tragedy rocked my world. My father had a massive heart attack, fell over, and died. My dad had always been my hero; he was my role model and "grounding." When he died, it was as though the ground was pulled out from under me. Overnight my drug use intensified. It stopped being merely a recreational or spiritual quest. It became an escape.

Death will touch each of us in our lifetime in one way or another, and the way we respond to it will change the way we decide to live. When my dad died, I had no idea how to handle the grief. As a consequence, I went off the deep end, spiraling out of control.

My dad's death surprised us all. He was only fifty-six but had made some poor health choices that ended up being fatal. His death taught me a couple of valuable life lessons. First of all was the realization that life is fragile. Secondly, because of my dad's death, I had a clear understanding that there are very real consequences to the various life choices we make.

THE CRASH AND BURN AND THE RE-BIRTH

My years in college are a blur to me today. It took me seven long years to graduate instead of the four years it should have taken. But it was during this season of my life that I took the strategies, skills, and discipline I'd developed and began to put them into practice in the business arena.

In some ways, my business career began while I was still in college. In my role of student government, I had the mentoring and guidance of many professors, deans, and even the college president. These were the years where I really learned how to lead, how to strategize toward meeting goals, and how to work with others, even those I didn't fully agree with.

It was soon after my father passed away that I applied for a receptionist job at an insurance company close to where I was living. During my interview, I think I failed every entrance exam I was given, including spelling, basic accounting skills, and even my proficiency using the now-extinct typewriter. I knew my chances of landing the job were slim, so I figured I had nothing to lose by going all in. I promised the boss, "If you give me this job, you will never regret it." He must've seen something in my eagerness because he gave me the job.

Since I was still in school, he gave me the flexibility to take a full class load even though he expected me to work a full-time job. I'd go to class, race to work, then go back to class. A typical day started around 7:00 a.m. and ended with my final night class around 9:00 p.m. I was ambitious and knew how to work hard.

By the time my junior year rolled around, I was burning the candle at both ends. I was working long hours, going to school, and maintaining an unhealthy social life. My self-destructive behavior, while previously hidden, was becoming more evident to those around me, including my boss, who could easily see that I was headed for a breakdown.

It wasn't long before I finally crashed and burned. I was hospitalized and put on a supervised drug treatment plan. A week after being released from the hospital, I lost my job.

It was during this season that a pastor from my past stepped back into my life. He had been watching and waiting from the background for just the right moment to intervene. And when I was feeling the most lost and alone, he stepped in. He could see my inevitable crash and had made arrangements for me to move into the home of a young couple willing to nurse me back to good health over a thirty-day period.

Because I had a lot of time on my hands, I gravitated toward the bookshelf in the couple's home. I spied a little book that caught my eye. Although I remember very little about the book as a whole, it was a single sentence that leapt up off the page and exploded inside me: "Trusting God is not a feeling; it's a decision."

To this point, I believed I had strayed too far from God, so far that I couldn't imagine a way back. Because of my drug use, I believed I had been "enlightened" and had an intimate knowledge of Truth. But since my crash, I was under no illusions; I knew my feelings were unreliable. I was unhappy and felt a deep sense of hopelessness and loss.

I read those words again, rolling them over in my mind. "Trusting in God is not a feeling, it's a decision." It occurred to me that the author of that book had unknowingly tossed me a lifeline. Trusting God was a decision I could choose to make, not because of but in spite of my feelings or my beliefs.

To move forward I was going to have to set my emotions, denial, excuses, and blame aside. Only then could I make a positive decision and follow through with it.

At the time, I was going through the medically supervised drug treatment program. I was prescribed high doses of anti-anxiety medications designed to offset the lingering consequences of my years of drug abuse. The doctors told me I would be on these medications indefinitely.

However, as I began to heal, I knew I could be free of the medications. I was determined to shake my dependence on even the anti-anxiety medications.

A SECOND CHANCE

Eventually the company that fired me gave me my receptionist job back. I re-entered school and was able to graduate . . . but barely. I finished with just enough credits and GPA to make it out.

My boss was the founder of the insurance company and a real character. He resembled a mob boss, chain-smoking cigars and telling stories about his Italian upbringing, which sounded like life inside another "Godfather" sequel.

He was a study in contrasts. On the one hand, he was demanding and harsh in his expectations of our performance, commitment, and allegiance to the company. But on the other hand, he was generous with his resources, time, and mentorship. He would often boast that he had trained and produced at least thirty-eight different millionaires. Even though I was only the receptionist, I made no secret of my desire to become Number Thirty-nine.

We were a small staff working at the company's corporate headquarters in Southern California, with new offices launching in various cities across America.

In every piece of correspondence that went out from our office, we proudly stated that our office hours were, "7:00 a.m. to 7:00 p.m., 7 days a week, 365 days a year to serve you!"

During my days in that office, my boss was always the first one in and the last one to leave. We knew for a fact that he spent many nights sleeping on the floor in his office. He was the one who answered those random phone calls that would come in on Sundays or holidays.

It was a lesson we all learned well. As each of us in turn left to launch satellite operations around the country, we became the ones sleeping on the floor and manning our offices "7:00 a.m. to 7:00 p.m., 7 days a week, 365 days a year to serve you."

It was not unusual for us to receive calls in the middle of the night from the boss, demanding our presence in the office conference room to review the status of a project or to listen to his latest business idea. These sessions could be rough. He would routinely challenge our choices and openly criticize how we spent our time or who we spent our time with. He either helped to "make you" or to "break you." It was a little like Navy SEAL training in that working with him included sleep deprivation and a lot of yelling. But it all served to stretch our limits. Looking back on it now, these were years of tremendous growth for me.

Through it all, he gave us the opportunity to rise within the company as fast as we were capable. Most significantly, my boss inspired me (and at least thirty-eight who had gone before me) to model his sound business principles and copy his tireless work ethic as we all eventually launched out and built our own multimillion-dollar companies.

In following the strategies and skills developed in my original plan, I learned to do my job as a receptionist exceptionally well. And working as the company receptionist offered an amazing unintended benefit. I was in the unique position to learn every other position within the company. I was diligent to keep a sharp eye out for any extra activities I might be able to volunteer for. It became my mission to build relationships at every level within the company.

No job was too small or insignificant, whether it was helping others meet their deadlines, taking clients to the airport, or representing the company at after-hour events. I saw these as opportunities for me to learn and build relationships and create influence.

LAUNCHING A NEW OPPORTUNITY

After volunteering and stepping forward to grab any available opportunities, I was poised and ready when the "big one" came along. My boss wanted to open an office in Bismarck, North Dakota—in the dead of winter. I felt my insides flip. I knew it would be a huge challenge, but I wanted the chance to open that office. So when my boss asked me what I wanted as a college graduation gift, I told him I wanted to head up the new North Dakota operation.

He actually agreed to let me pursue it. Of course, that was partly because no one else was willing to go. The option of leaving Southern California and moving to North Dakota was pretty bleak. After some discussion, my boss gave me the go-ahead. He told me to go home, pack up, and be at the office on the following Thursday morning. He promised to have the company car serviced, filled with gas, and ready to go. He also told me he'd have a check ready to cover my travel and re-location expenses.

I came to the office bright and early Thursday, ready to begin my adventure. But my boss was nowhere to be found. There was no money or company credit card waiting for me. The company car had not been serviced. I waited all morning and through the lunch hour for him to show up. By that afternoon he'd still not returned my calls or checked into the office.

Rather than miss the opportunity to launch a new market and manage my own operation, I mustered all my confidence and stormed into my boss's office, taking the keys to the company car off the hook on the wall. I put all my things in the car and made my way directly to the bank, where I withdrew all my life savings, a whopping $250. With that done, I headed out of town on my very first solo road trip.

I was exhilarated! I was on my way to North Dakota to launch the company's brand-new branch office. I felt I was not only launching a new office, I was launching my career!

Moving from Newport Beach, California, to Bismarck, North Dakota, was an adventure indeed. I was separated from my family and all that was familiar for the very first time in my life.

I discovered that the contrasts between Southern California's coast and the ranches and farmland of North Dakota were significant, to say the least. Locals proudly wore Wranglers instead of Levis, boots instead of flip-flops, cowboy hats instead of visors. Even the pickup trucks were more valuable and popular in North Dakota than the prominent BMWs and Mercedes you'd find along the California coastal roads.

The values I had been raised to follow as a child were easier for me to grasp because they were far more commonly held in North Dakota than in Southern California. Spiritual and business principles became dynamic and applicable truths as I saw them illustrated daily on the farms and ranches surrounding Bismarck.

The lives of the people were rooted in the land and in the weather. Their lifestyle revolved around laws of nature like sowing seeds and reaping harvests, and every seed planted producing fruit after its own kind. Even the seasons of the year were a new thing for me. These were laws of success I could grasp, follow, and understand because they were displayed before me in the lifestyle of the people I rubbed shoulders with every day.

I spent most weekends during those North Dakota years living on the Circle C Ranch, which was owned by a singing evangelist and rodeo chaplain. She became a valuable spiritual mentor to me during that time in my life. While at the ranch I got to take care of and ride the horses, work on the ranch, work a rodeo, and do things other Southern California kids only see in the movies. Those years were an incredibly fun season of my life.

Experiences like the move to North Dakota formed the basis of the AUDIT Principle. Leaving the security of home to go to a new state with only $250 in my pocket built my faith in incredible ways. That move taught me to love the adventures life brings my way. North Dakota was my first big step of faith in business.

ANOTHER STEP IN THE JOURNEY

After successfully starting and managing the North Dakota company for two years, I was offered another opportunity. This one to relocate to Albuquerque, New Mexico, to take over and revive the company's struggling New Mexico operations. It was a new season in the evolution of the company, and my boss urged me to accept.

With each new move, I was keenly aware of my fragile health and made the decision early on to do two important things upon arrival. The first was to find a doctor who would monitor and manage my medical condition. The other was to identify and engage in a local church. The rest of my attention was focused on my work of building the business, which I enjoyed and was good at.

Each doctor in each new state agreed with the initial prognosis, deeming it important for me to continue the medical treatment plan. At the same time, each church I attended taught a message of finding freedom in overcoming life's obstacles. Throughout those years, I spent hundreds of hours driving to business meetings and listening to inspirational and motivational tapes. I was continually exposed to positive words that reinforced the message that life's opportunities are without limitations. The more I learned that I could be free from the consequences of my past, the more persuaded I became that I could get off the medications.

It was while living in Albuquerque that my pastor and his wife agreed to have me move into their home with the objective of helping me get off the prescribed medications. After months of considering this step, I was finally serious about this process and decided on the "cold turkey" strategy, stopping all the medications at once.

Battling the severe symptoms of withdrawal was the most physically, psychologically, and spiritually challenging experience I'd ever lived through. It was a full week of violent physical reactions, extreme chills, vomiting, aches, pains, and hallucinations.

About three days into the experience I felt like I was losing my mind. I could feel the line between reality and delusion beginning to slip. I couldn't sleep and spent my days and nights either pacing the floor or sitting in a recliner.

It was in that time of desperation that I realized there was only one truth that mattered to me anymore. I spoke out loud, "God, either you are or you're not, and if you are, you are everything you say you are. But if you are not, then life doesn't matter anymore." I meant it. I was either going to depend on Him and get well or I was prepared to die right then and there.

That night, I made the decision to believe that He was everything He said He was, and I staked my life on it. Since that moment, I have lived my life based on this premise.

4

MY LIFE WITH DAVID

MOVING TO UTAH

BY THE TIME I entered my fifth year with the company, I was ready for a change. In a few short years, I had moved from Southern California to North Dakota and now to Albuquerque. And while I was originally energized by the new challenges, I had grown restless and ready for something different.

I heard through the grapevine that Salt Lake City was on a short list of viable locations for a new branch of my company. Utah is a beautiful place, famous for its mountain ranges, national parks, and wide-open spaces. But it's also famous for being the world headquarters for the Mormon faith, centering in the beautiful Mormon Tabernacle located on Temple Square in downtown Salt Lake City.

Mormons are known for being a devout people, deeply rooted in their faith with strong principles and an abiding belief in church and family. But their tight-knit communities can sometimes feel exclusive and even mysterious to outsiders. Because of this perception, the company's strategy was to hire managers for this new branch from within Utah's prominent faith community.

With this goal in mind, the company prepared a detailed profile for what they believed would be their ideal candidate. They were looking for a good-looking male in his mid-thirties who held an active role within the faith community. He would have spent two years serving on a mission, as most Mormon high school graduates do. The devotion to faith would be critically important, as would the sales skills he would have developed while sharing his faith door-to-door. In addition, the company felt that knowing a second language would be an asset.

In theory, hiring a local resident who has established relationships within a state certainly makes good sense. However, being a startup operation, the company needed a director who was self-motivated and able to manage the business with little or no direct supervision. The position needed to be filled by an individual who knew the company's services and culture inside and out, someone who could step directly into the market and quickly launch the company's brand and its products. They needed a director with perseverance, someone who was committed to achieving the company's goals regardless of the challenges, obstacles, and time constraints.

After three failed attempts to find just the right person for the job, the company turned their attention to me. They had taken notice of my successes in North Dakota and New Mexico and they were aware of my desire for a new challenge. Surprisingly, I was disappointed when they offered me the position because I was not very interested in leaving Albuquerque. However, I had learned that promotion often requires a location change, so I quickly set my sights on Utah and began planning my move.

It didn't take long for me to get the lay of the land. I realized that if I wanted to be a success in Utah, which is a strong community-based state, I was going to need to boldly step into that community, committed to being a contributing member. This would require me to develop some new skills. I'm not a naturally born extrovert, so it's tough for me to "work a room," shaking hands with strangers, learning names and making new friends. But if I wanted to be a success in this new position, I would have to get out of my comfort zone and learn to become much more outgoing.

Although the culture and geography were unique, the principles for success were the same in Utah as in other places I'd lived and worked. Job One was to become educated in the community. Who were the "movers and shakers?" Who were the leaders, the ones who always seemed to be involved in the projects that succeeded? These were the people I needed to get to know. I needed to become educated in the community. What made it tick? What were its values, what was important?

I was committed to volunteering and serving within the community, building relationships and therefore building influence. I knew from experience that the greatest sales and business opportunities would come through the relationships I was able to build.

Utah possesses one of the strongest economies and business climates in the nation. It has enjoyed the lowest unemployment in the country and continues to be featured in business magazines as one of the top states both for living and starting a business.

Yet I've known many business people who have relocated to Salt Lake City only to leave months later. When asked about it, they'll admit their discouragement. They tell me they just couldn't fit in; they couldn't crack through the community and do business as an outsider.

But I discovered not being able to do business as an outsider is at best a myth, and at worst, an excuse. And we've already talked about how excuses can thwart forward movement. There are huge advantages to stepping into a brand-new area. You can recreate your personal brand, your persona. You have the chance to start over and build a brand-new reputation.

In my case, I was shy and introverted, but I could now choose to be outgoing and fun! No one in Utah knew the old me, so I could rebuild my personality. I could be anything I chose to be. I could be dynamic, energetic, and approachable. Like karate years before, all it took was practice. Practice and a lot of hard work.

Not a day goes by that I'm not thankful for being sent to this magnificent land, often called "Zion" by the locals. But for me, it's a different Biblical reference that comes to mind when I think of my adopted home: "Eden." Utah has been a place of abundance and blessing for me. Whether because of its beauty, its people, or its opportunities in education, business, and recreation, Utah is the perfect spot for me. From the start I was impressed by Utah's outstanding and engaged citizens, always friendly and embracing.

After growing up in Southern California and moving to North Dakota as well as other locales, I would've never guessed that Utah would become my final relocation. In Utah I experienced my greatest challenges and successes while having the opportunity to contribute at levels I only dreamed of. Utah represents a place where my faith was tested beyond what I could have imagined. Utah is where I purchased my very first home and it's where I met David, who became the center of my world.

MEETING DAVID

When I arrived in Salt Lake City, my first order of business was to find a church where I could belong. Notice I said "belong" and not "attend." As you no doubt know by now, I'm a big believer in community. I believe that a vibrant church is a wonderful place to find new friends and a supportive community.

Before arriving in Utah, I learned about a unique little non-denominational church holding unconventional services in an old converted mechanic's garage. The church was called "The Full Armor" and used the car bays as the nursery, classrooms, office, and "living room," which was kind of an informal gathering space. It sounded like my kind of place. When I first visited the city, I purposefully chose a hotel close to the garage. My first night in town I decided to give the garage a try. I was ready to dive into my new outgoing personality and figured that the garage might be a good place for a trial run. That night I had an experience I'll never forget.

The pastor, Jim, was a tough guy, the son of a moonshiner,

ex-military, ex-firefighter, just the kind of person you might expect to head up a church that met in a garage. But as a pastor he was one of the kindest, gentlest men I've ever known. He shepherded a diverse group of folks that included businessmen, firefighters, a NASA engineer, and a judge. Add to that mix several dozen young people, and you have a very interesting congregation.

Also in this diverse crowd was a small group of rough-looking characters. One of them in particular, a biker by the look of him, caught my eye. It was in the garage's living room where I first met David. He was different from anyone I'd ever met. He was gregarious, bold, charismatic, and well on his way to becoming a much-sought-after speaker and minister. He was tall and handsome, yet when you looked beneath his shirt sleeves, the prison tattoos and scars were evidence that he had lived a violent and troubled past.

After just a few minutes of visiting, I could easily tell that our backgrounds couldn't have been more different. Whereas I grew up surrounded by influence and wealth, living on the upper "Back Bay" of Newport Beach, David had grown up in East Los Angeles, in a barrio not far from Watts, famous for the riots that destroyed much of the town in the 70s and then again after the trial of Rodney King in the early 90s. Each home in David's LA neighborhood had bars across their windows and multiple deadbolt locks on their doors. Every door, that is, except David's.

I was riveted as he told me about his widowed mother, who refused to put bars in her windows, believing it would be an admission that she had lost the battle and given up title to her home. Even though I hadn't met her yet, I was impressed with this woman's bravery and tenacity. She refused to give in to the gangs and crime that surrounded her little home.

That night David kept me spellbound with stories about his growing up years, usually centering on his mother. She was known all over the neighborhood as "Big Red." But it wasn't because of her size; it was her personality that earned her that nickname. He told me when he was a boy, a teacher from school scratched his face. David's mom, who was only five feet tall, armed herself with a baseball bat and chased that teacher down to teach him a lesson. She stopped short of beating the teacher, but the nickname remained. She was a legend all through the neighborhood.

David sported multiple tattoos, rode a Harley Davidson with notorious biker clubs, and spent time in two different prisons. But by the time I met him that evening in the garage, the tattoos and tough exterior no longer defined the man he had become.

What I didn't know that first night in the garage was that roughly a year before, David had made his own way to the Full Armor. Before he knew it, he was in the middle of a life-changing conversation with Jim, who could relate to David in a way that very few men in the ministry could. As fun as it was to hear David relate that first experience, it was always great to hear it from the pastor's point of view. Jim said, "I didn't know if we were going to have a fist fight that night or not. I found myself face-to-face with this angry young man, challenging him in a way that I'd never challenged anyone before. I told him he wasn't man enough to change, that he didn't have the guts to live a meaningful life of purpose and love. At that point, David grabbed me by the shirt collar, lifted me off the ground and shouted, 'Yes I am!'"

David told his side of the story. "I didn't understand what was happening. I searched out that garage because I was told the pastor had answers to questions I was wrestling with. One minute we're talking when suddenly I had the pastor by his shirt collar, shouting at him, his face just inches from mine. Once I was able to calm down, the two of us agreed to resume the conversation the next day. But as I drove away that night, I had to pull my car to the curb because I couldn't see through my tears. When I was finally able to compose myself and pull away, I knew I was forever changed."

Through the months ahead, David spent every day and night hanging out at the garage. They had even given him his own key so he could stop by whenever he wasn't working at his roofing job. The congregation immediately adopted him as their own, and David found himself being mentored and fed by this unique and diverse group of men and women. Before long he was telling his dramatic story at businessmen's luncheons and speaking at Sunday services around town.

After a few days of getting the lay of the land in Salt Lake City, I returned home to New Mexico to settle my affairs and prepare for my move. Once back in Albuquerque, I packed up all my worldly goods in a small U-Haul and returned to Salt Lake City to move into the apartment I'd put a deposit on during my scouting trip. Sensing the beginning of a potential relationship, Jim from the Full Armor sent David over to help me unload the U-Haul and move in. That was all it took. Over the next couple of weeks, we spent every spare moment together. We became best friends and eventually got engaged. A short six months later, we were married.

A LIFE TOGETHER

Looking back, I see this season of our lives together as fun and carefree. David worked his roofing job as I continued to build the company's Utah operations. Evenings and weekends were dedicated to recreation and developing our speaking skills, both as a couple and as individuals. Before long, organizations began inviting us to be their keynote speakers. A local TV station asked us to host a weekly talk show. Even though we chose to only host a few shows, we learned something from the experience. We learned that we presented a unique dynamic that people were attracted to. "The biker and the business woman," described us as a couple who could reach a diverse audience. Our message was one of "Potential, Increase, and Abundance." The encouragement to every group we spoke to was that if we could succeed, with all our differences, anyone could.

We bought a home and about a year later gave birth to our son, Jonathan. With the responsibility of a new baby, we decided that David would quit his job to stay home with Jonny. This would allow him time to begin the ground-breaking work of building a new non-profit organization dedicated to helping others overcome adversity, experience freedom, and achieve success. My job would provide income and health care benefits until we were able to launch our new non-profit.

I loved being David's partner in ministry. His stories, humor, and energy combined with his strong physical and charismatic presence conveyed a combination of credibility and compassion that captivated audiences. My role in the narrative was to share on topics like overcoming adversities and gaining new levels of success by learning how to apply specific laws and principles.

Our messages and personal growth developed as we studied scripture, laws of science, and other tested principles and then applied them to our own life situations and stories. There were "aha" moments every time we answered the big "why" questions. We did this by being able to tie a specific action or series of actions to a corresponding principle, law, or scripture.

We often took long drives listening to tapes by motivational and spiritual leaders like Zig Ziegler, Anthony Robbins, and Norman Vincent Peal. Sometimes during these road trips we would randomly assign each other a topic and then take turns delivering an impromptu five-minute message to the other on that topic. Afterward we'd critique each other's message. We were always intentional about identifying the principle or law that supported each premise given in the message. The AUDIT Principle was hammered out in the early days on those long car trips with David.

We discovered that when we identified the principles and laws at work and applied them to our lives, we experienced results far beyond what we'd known was possible. Our common exclamation to each other became, "Oh my gosh, this stuff actually works!"

We saw life as a walk of faith and embraced the saying, "If you can believe it, you can achieve it." Our definition of the word "belief" wasn't passive. It included strong elements of action and life application. We were fully aware that we were in a season of growth and learning. Life was an adventure! Every experience, every situation and circumstance, was guiding us through transition toward our ultimate destiny.

Our dream as a couple echoed my mission as a young girl:

To go where few people went and touch lives others didn't touch. This dream filled us with passion and empathy toward communities within unique demographics. We were an unlikely union to be sure, but we were fully persuaded that we'd been brought together and led forward by divine forces.

We made a plan and pursued it daily. Debt and other baggage that we'd brought to our marriage was tackled and conquered. We were fully engaged in each other, our marriage, and our life together.

I continued to work hard and was rewarded with promotions. David spent his days writing, studying, and building considerable relationships within the community with our son Jonny always close by, on his lap or on his shoulders.

WHAT A DIFFERENCE A DAY MAKES

Then in a single day, with no notice or time to prepare, life suddenly changed course. David made an emergency trip to the hospital for treatment of what he thought was a pulled muscle or a pinched nerve. After looking at an x-ray, the doctors in the emergency room believed it was something far more serious like pneumonia. When David's condition failed to improve over time, we knew it was something else and were referred to an oncologist. After examining him and running some tests, the doctor told us David had terminal bone and lung cancer. Further, he told us that the cancer was invasive and too far along for effective treatment. We were sent home that day with no encouragement and no hope, with the words "there's not much time" echoing in our ears.

As the doctor gave us his prognosis, I felt like collapsing, but David didn't flinch. I remember David simply folding me into his arms and declaring, "Jane Ann, we're going to beat this." I believed him.

That began an eight-month journey where David and I faced our fears and fought the good fight together. The thinner and weaker David became, the more our friends and neighbors rallied around us. They supported us with meals, encouragement, and fellowship. David continued to take care of Jonny, now almost two years old, while I continued to work, providing the much-needed health insurance and finances.

Before leaving for my job each day, I would strategically place notes all over the house crafted to encourage and coach David along, reminding him that he was going to win this battle. I wanted him to know that he was not going to die but live a long life, fulfilling his God-given destiny.

In the seventh month, three remarkable women took turns staying with David while I continued to work. Day after day, they walked with David and Jonathan, made lunch, cleaned the house, and spent precious hours talking and laughing with David until I could get home, which got earlier and earlier as the days progressed. Finally, I knew in my heart that it was time to call David's mom, Florene, who was gracious enough to come and live with us those final few weeks.

ANGELS AMONG US?

It was early fall, and the trees in our backyard were heavy with fruit. Along with the beautiful weather and ripe fruit on the trees came the nectar-seeking wasps—yellow jackets to be precise.

Almost overnight we were overwhelmed with yellow jackets. David, Jonny, and Florene were unable to enjoy the patio because the yellow jackets were everywhere. The yellow jackets were not content to stay outside; they were getting into the house.

Finances were tight, so I delayed trying to do anything about the problem. I slept little, increasingly more aware of the possibility that David might not make it much longer. I was tired and my faith and hope were fading, which frightened me. Any other time I would have looked at the wasps as a simple nuisance. But with everything else going on, the wasps represented something much more sinister. They finally got so bad that Florene called the exterminators.

That day I came home from work and found David lying on the living room sofa sleeping. As I watched him sleep, my heart broke at how weak and frail he had become. Fighting back the tears, I didn't know how long I could maintain my composure. If I couldn't stand strong for him, who would? It was in this moment that the doorbell rang.

I opened my front door to find an elderly Greek man with unruly white curly hair wearing an exterminator's uniform. I did my best to force a smile and attempted to muster up a greeting, thanking him for coming. As I stumbled over my words, the man stood still on the doorstep. With genuine compassion, he took my hand and quietly asked, "What's wrong, honey?"

After months of "standing strong" and never letting my guard down, believing David's life depended upon my strength, I finally broke down and the tears freely flowed. This kind exterminator demonstrated a fatherly affection, walking me back into our house. He sat by David and encouraged me and loved us.

Over the next few weeks, this kind man not only eliminated the yellow jacket problem, he called and checked up on us just to see how we were doing. He continued to check in on us even after David's death. To this day, I've never received a bill for his services. I often wonder if that kind Greek man wasn't an exterminator at all, but an angel sent from Heaven to bring us encouragement.

CODE BLUE

It was mid-morning when David's mom called me at work with the news, "Jane Ann, David had me call an ambulance for him. He's having a hard time breathing. Can you meet him at the hospital?" I immediately gathered my things and drove to the hospital, arriving at the same time as the ambulance carrying my husband.

As David sat on the gurney behind the curtain, the doctor took me aside. I braced myself, not wanting to hear whatever it was he had to tell me. He wanted me to allow the hospital to withhold oxygen from David. I was stunned. I knew David was sitting just on the other side of the curtain, alert but suffering, relying on me to work with the doctors on his behalf to expedite some much-needed relief. And yet the doctor was telling me to withhold the very thing that David so desperately needed. In effect, the doctor was asking me to agree to his imposed death sentence.

I adamantly argued against the doctor's suggestion. "No

way! David is alert and frightened. He's not ready to die. He just needs the oxygen!"

So the doctor reluctantly prescribed the oxygen and ordered a bed and room for David. Later that night the hospital speaker system came alive with the words, "Code Blue, Code Blue!" From every direction, doctors, nurses, and attendants with their defibrillator cart all came running. They raced into his room in response to David's cardiac arrest. Although they were successful in resuscitating him, David fell into a coma that night and never recovered.

Ironically, the same doctor from the emergency room was assigned to David as his attending physician. As this doctor watched me sit by David's bed, quietly talking to my unresponsive husband about our future together, he became more and more concerned about my mental and emotional state of being.

For those three days, I refused to accept not only the hospital chaplain's counsel but also the counsel of the social worker. They both tried to convince me that there was no hope. Finally, after three days, the doctor could no longer stay silent. He felt compelled to express his concern to me. "Jane Ann, the nurses and I are afraid that you are in denial, refusing to accept the fact that your husband is dying. It's time to acknowledge the truth of David's condition."

JUST A HAND'S LENGTH AWAY

It was in that moment that a famous Bible story taught every year in my childhood Sunday school classes came rushing back to mind. It was the dramatic narrative of Jesus's disciples fearfully battling the wind and waves of a torrential storm as they attempted to control their boat while crossing the lake. As the water violently splashed over the boat's gunwales, making it almost impossible to see, those on the boat looked up to see what appeared to be a ghost walking on the surface of the water. However, one of the men, Peter, realized that the image coming toward him was not a ghost at all; it was Jesus Christ Himself, walking on the water.

For a moment, boldness rose up within Peter, and he called out, "Lord, if it is you, tell me to come to you on the water." Jesus told Peter to come, so he climbed out of the boat and miraculously walked across the water. However, as he got only a hand-length away from Jesus, he became distracted by the wind and began to sink. In the story, Jesus immediately reached out and took Peter by the hand, saying to him, "Why did you doubt? Why do you have so little faith?"

Even as a kid, every time I heard this story, I wondered why Jesus chastized Peter for having so little faith. Peter had just climbed out of a boat in a torrential storm and did the impossible; he walked on the water! That sounds like quite a bit of faith to me.

Now, as the doctor was trying to persuade me to give up my hope, I found my mind drifting further into this Bible story and its current relevance to me. With an unexpected and profound clarity, I responded to the physician, "Doctor, do you remember the story of Jesus walking on the water?"

Rolling his eyes with obvious exasperation, he nodded his head. With that simple backdrop of understanding, I quietly explained, "I don't want to be like Peter who, in the middle of a miracle only a hand's length away from Jesus, began to sink because he took his eyes off the Lord and started to worry about the storm. So, thank you for your concern, but I'm not in denial. I just need to see this all the way through."

In a heartbeat, all of his tension and frustration dissipated. He took a breath and paused before declaring, "I can work with that." He suddenly understood that I had chosen to believe all the way to the end.

David never recovered from his coma. Of course, I was devastated. But I never had to endure the thoughts that might have tormented me like, "Why didn't I give David a chance to live? Why did I withhold the oxygen that he needed so desperately?" Or "Was David's healing just a hand's length away?"

Since David's death, I've learned that every miracle and success story includes challenges and obstacles that test our faith and endurance. Too many people quit "just a hand's length away." As Napoleon Hill wrote in his famous book, *Think and Grow Rich*, after interviewing hundreds of the world's most innovative and successful businessmen, "More than 500 of the most successful men this country has ever known told the author their greatest success came just one step beyond the point at which defeat had overtaken them. Failure is a trickster with a keen sense of irony and cunning. It takes great delight in tripping one when success is almost within reach."

WHAT NOW?

Faced with the reality that I was a single parent, I found myself asking the same questions other single parents ask themselves:

"Who will watch my son while I'm at work? How can I afford daycare? Who will take my son to school and pick him up each day? Will he still be able to play team sports like soccer and basketball? Will my son still be able to live a normal life?"

The answers to these questions eluded me. Before, whenever I struggled with difficult questions, I always had my partner by my side. Together we were able to find a solution. Nothing made me feel so alone as realizing that David wasn't there to help me figure out the answers to these questions.

Like I learned from my own loving parents, I knew what I wanted for me and my son; I just wasn't sure how I was going to be able to accomplish it. I wanted to be an engaged and "present" mom, taking my child to school each day and chaperoning his field trips. I wanted to be that mom who cheered on her son from the bleachers at each of his games and performances. I wanted to take him on camping trips, enroll him in scouting, and provide him with many of the experiences other boys would have growing up. I wanted to make sure he had all the security, benefits, and experiences that childhood had to offer.

We had a great deal of support from friends who included us in their family outings and accompanied us on our weekend adventures. Without me knowing it, a couple of David's friends had vowed they would be there for us, teaching Jonny "man skills" and helping me with tasks that David had previously handled. These men took their commitment seriously, showing up to shovel snow, deliver firewood, and "rough and tumble" with my son.

One particular family took Jonny in, treating him as their

third son while I went to work each day. This wonderful family added a sense of security and support, providing him with two older siblings. But as he prepared to enter kindergarten, it became more difficult for these parents, who were already struggling to juggle their own family needs, to add another child to their routine.

My job also required more and more of my time and attention. The company continued to promote me, expanding my territory, staff, and responsibilities. And with each promotion came a raise, rewarding my efforts and giving hope to future financial freedom. But there was a downside. My promotions and increased responsibilities demanded more travel and more time away from my son.

Although the company had served me well over the years, a conflicted restlessness and sense of urgency was growing within me. Although the company had provided a great career, my circumstances had changed. It was hard to accept that something I enjoyed so much didn't serve my future. It was a new thought that the company might no longer be the right vehicle to get me where I wanted to go.

LIFE IS AN ADVENTURE!

Once again, the need to make changes bubbled up inside me. I was on the threshold of a whole new adventure. And isn't that what life is—an adventure?

Adventures are dangerous and exciting with surprises around every bend. But they're not always fun. They can be terrifying and exhausting. But there is joy in the journey itself, not just in arriving at the destination.

I was about midway in the journey home from a short business trip when I found myself on a stretch of road that I had first traveled years earlier when I arrived in Utah. I had been driving for hours through a barren desert landscape when the road began to elevate. I continued up the winding road until I was able to look down on the valley below.

Like an oasis, there was a beautiful community of small farms all situated neatly in the shade of the majestic Rocky Mountains looming in the east. I remembered the unexpected delight I felt as I became consumed with an indescribable joy. I was full of anticipation of the new life and promise of adventure that lay before me.

Now here I was again, driving that same stretch of road. I reached the same summit and was greeted with the same view of the valley below. In a moment, I relived every emotion I experienced years before when life was a promise and a dream waiting to be fulfilled.

Suddenly, like an uncontrollable flash flood, a suffocating wave of disappointment overtook me. My life was no longer a promise. My dreams were in ruins, and the life I thought was in front of me was over. All my dreams and goals and visions had died along with David. Now what was going to happen to me?

The next evening, I had dinner with two of my closest friends and mentors. We sat in a secluded booth in my favorite restaurant located in one of Utah's famous ski resorts, just minutes from my home. I shared with them my recent road trip experience at the top of the mountain.

I couldn't get through the story without my emotions

welling up. Through tears, I struggled to say, "I remember when life was such an adventure—"

Before I could finish my sentence, my wise friend interrupted with a gentle smile and said, "No, Jane Ann, now you are discovering what an adventure life really is."

The best adventures aren't planned at all. That's what makes them adventures!

5

STARTING MY COMPANY

T HE THREE YEARS following David's death were intense. Losing David was devastating, and I had to work especially hard to pursue spiritual healing and healthy self-development. I was focused on making sure Jonny experienced a happy and full childhood while serving within our community and growing the company's footprint in Utah.

Although I believe I hid it well from Jonny, my coworkers, and those around me, I continued to struggle with grief and disappointment, maybe even a sense of failure. David's death was never part of any plan we'd made. I was restless and wondered what the next chapter in my life would involve.

A friend of mine helped me stop striving to find meaning in why David died. This friend helped me move on and pursue a destiny of my own. With his help, I accepted that David's death might be something I would never fully understand.

To help me grasp the value of this truth, he told me a story about General Douglas MacArthur and his brilliant plan to re-take the islands of the Philippines. His plan entailed "leapfrogging." He said, "We won't fight where the Japanese are strong. We'll leap over the top of them. We won't take the populated islands."

As I listened to this story, I realized there are some islands I simply cannot take. Up until that point I assumed that I had to "take every island," conquer all my obstacles, understand everything in order to move forward. But that day I realized there are times when we have to let go, and this was one of those times. I had to let go of the things I couldn't understand and move on to my own calling and destiny.

From that day on, anytime those negative thoughts hit me, I would declare to myself, "I'm off to the Philippines!"

DÉJÀ VU

One day I was standing in my kitchen pondering these things after a long day at work. My mind wandered from subject to subject, not really settling on any one thing. From my vantage point, I could look out through the sliding glass window into the back yard. I could turn in the other direction and see out the front door into the street that passed in front of the house.

Immediately, I had a déjà vu moment. I remembered standing in David's hospital room the day he died and looking out into the hallway. I remember being struck by the hustle and bustle that was going on just past the threshold of the room, people rushing by, oblivious to my pain and the devastation it caused me.

Now gazing out into the street, I was struck once again by the busyness of the world going on just outside my door. Although my world had frozen in place, the world around me continued to swirl without a thought or care as to how I felt or what I was doing.

That day in the hospital, I knew I was going to have to cross the threshold into a world without David. Now looking out my front door, I was faced with the very same realization. I was looking through another portal into another decision I was going to have to make, another line I was going to have to cross.

STEPPING INTO THE UNKNOWN

The feeling was so intense and profound that I recognized it as a call to action. I was being challenged to take another step, and it was going to have to be a deliberate one. It was time for me to make a decision to change. I didn't hear an audible voice from God, but in that instant, I knew it was time for me to leave my job. It was time for me to step into the great big vast unknown.

I made the decision to start an insurance company. I would build a company to sell for millions of dollars. This company would become the vehicle I would use to get to my destination. It would support my goals, dreams, and visions.

I knew I needed to move quickly before I could change my mind. With that thought, I ran directly to my home office and typed a hurried resignation letter, then raced to the local Fed Ex office, where I sent the letter overnight to my boss in another city. I returned home and immediately called him to deliver my thirty-day notice.

When my boss received my official notice letter, he flew to Salt Lake City and met me at the office. He did all he could to try to get me to stay with the company. I was very clear that the reason I was leaving had nothing to do with the company itself. I wanted to pursue other avenues that would allow me to be more available for my son. The more we talked, the more desperate he became to keep me.

Finally, just to get away from his barrage, I got up and went into the ladies' room. But even that didn't stop him. He followed me in!

Next it was the HR director's turn. She did what she could do to sway me. Even the president of the company flew into town to encourage me to stay. He offered me more money and more opportunity. But I was convinced it was time for me to leave. I was clear on my new purpose and direction.

After the thirty-day notice was up, I woke up to my very first day of being unemployed. I was never tempted to call and beg for my job back. The new-found freedom was exhilarating and refreshing. It was the first time since high school that I'd been without work, and it was weird not having a job or any-place to go. But the page had turned, and I was ready. It was time for a new vehicle.

ANOTHER BUSINESS PLAN

It was Memorial Day weekend and because of the break, I had made arrangements for my brother to fly up and help me construct a business plan—the second business plan of my life. But this plan would be very different than the one I wrote in high school. It would need to be much more than a couple of columns listed on a legal pad and would require a lot more thought and expertise. I needed all the help I could get and was glad my brother had agreed to walk with me through the process.

Like any business plan, this one would have to put into words the vision and blueprint for my company. The plan needed to spell out my strategy for starting, growing, and taking the company to a successful acquisition. It was also going to have to answer all the questions potential investors were going to have, not only questions like, "Why do you want to start a company?" but more importantly, "Why should I invest? What's in it for me?"

I needed the business plan to not only be a distillation of my vision; I needed it to be an effective tool to raise money. I was a widowed single mother with very few resources available to invest into my new venture. If my dream of starting a company was to have a fighting chance, I needed an infusion of cash. I saw the business plan as a critical tool in my hands to raise the money.

David and I had been a young married couple filled with dreams, optimism, and faith, but our bank accounts were far from full. David came into our marriage with quite a lot of debt, and every dime we saved went to pay off that debt. My financial desperation was especially evident the morning after he died. Before I could even make funeral arrangements, I had to stop by our local Sears to borrow $500 on my credit card to cover the initial burial costs.

In the three years since David's death, I was able to provide a comfortable living for my son and me, but I was not making nearly enough money to build back any significant savings. Quitting my job certainly didn't help! I had stepped off the cliff into an immediately difficult situation. With very little savings to fall back on, I needed money quickly. Not only enough to meet our daily needs but enough to start and support a business that would bring the investors their promised return.

I felt like a kid on the first day of school. I got my pad of paper and my pen and I situated myself comfortably on the floor at my coffee table. I prepared to write the perfect business plan. I had mentally written this document hundreds of times before while in the shower or on a run or in the middle of a workout, but now as I stared down at the blank page, I had no idea where to start.

As I sat on the floor gazing at the pad of paper in front of me, my brother walked into my living room and immediately noticed the "deer in the headlights" expression on my face. It was clear that I had no idea what I was doing. Rather than sympathize with me or pat me on the head, he told me to get myself to the nearest bookstore and buy a couple of books on how to write a business plan!

I got up from my place on the floor and made my way to the mall. The change of scenery was a positive thing. Getting up and out of the house and having a distraction helped me gain some much-needed perspective. I found the books I needed and headed back home. Armed with two very simple and descriptive instruction manuals, I was ready to do battle with that blank sheet of paper.

An exciting wave of momentum followed as my vision came to life. Something magical happens when you take the time to think about your vision, plan it out, and finally put it into words. You're putting the idea into a form that others can catch and run with. It's fulfilling to see what was once just a dream in your head take shape in black and white on the page.

Once I had my goals down, the words flowed a little easier. It was like breaking the seal on a bottle. All those dreams I had shelved found new life as they tumbled onto the paper.

Although I considered a few other career directions, I knew that the best course of action was to start a company (build a vehicle) using the skills I already possessed, skills that had been developed in the insurance industry over the past sixteen years.

In my previous job, I had worked my way up all the way from the company receptionist to a sales director, gaining skills and building new relationships each step of the way. Rather than learn something new, I made the important decision to build a company in the insurance industry.

A MAP TO A NEW DESTINATION

When that Memorial Day weekend began, I was an unemployed, single mom saddled with a great deal of trepidation and the haunting second thoughts that accompany any great adventure. But now, after almost a week of planning and writing, a transition was taking place, something powerful was happening. There was now a plan, and that plan was written down, in words, on paper. I buzzed with a whole new level of energy. It was almost unbelievable; I was going to build my own company!

I had taken the seed of an idea and developed it into a plan. Now there was a map to follow. This was a major building block, and not just for the creation of the company. This building block was another big piece of the AUDIT Principle.

The plan laid out the strategy, the vision for the company, but it was also a tangible explanation of a compelling investment opportunity to share with potential shareholders. Raising money would be no easy feat. The opportunity I was pitching to potential investors was a highly regulated financial institution. The plan was ambitious, calling for building the company over a three- to five-year period and eventually selling it for millions of dollars.

Many of the investors invested in me as a person much more than investing in my business plan. I couldn't afford to wow potential investors with a beautiful brochure complete with 4-color art on heavy bonded paper. My written plan was much more basic than that, just a short stack of copy paper pages stapled together.

But the format of the plan wasn't nearly as important as the plan itself, the story I was telling them. These investors were connecting with my passion as I related to them the "verbal narrative" of the dream of the new company. But it was the actual writing down that was critical. Without the discipline to go through the process of putting the plan on paper, there would've been no way to effectively communicate the narrative.

The goal wouldn't just be about the destination. The real adventure would come in the journey along the way. However, I couldn't lose sight of goals that I had set. These goals drove me, and I was determined not to fail. Like I learned as a young girl, there's value in seeing the end from the beginning. I was able to live life intentionally and with a sense of urgency.

Just like any great adventure, there would be the unexpected delays and detours, collisions and tickets, shortcuts and sight-seeing, new relationships and unforgettable experiences. But I was on my way, and it was exhilarating.

From its genesis, my plan was to build a company and to sell it. And although the company began as a vehicle to support my goals, dreams, and visions, it didn't take long to discover that building a business was much bigger and more significant than simply meeting my family's needs and goals. It served to meet the goals and dreams of countless others.

Over the years the company has provided training and careers, health benefits, education, and resources for hundreds of employees. It has supported and helped to grow local vendors and continues to serve its communities. It served to give me as well as many others a voice of influence and the resources to contribute to our community, to causes we are passionate about.

My business plan projected three to five years to start and bring the company to a successful acquisition. But instead, it took fifteen years, fifteen challenging and wonderful years. Isn't it often that way? I think that if we could see all that our journey will take at the beginning, many of us would never start!

And as with any venture, there were challenges that seemed insurmountable, successes that still amaze me, and relationships that made every challenge an adventure to look back on with pride and camaraderie. There was the mundane daily grind but there was also the frequent, "Hold on tight, here comes another curve!"

Building the company gave me the opportunity to be surrounded every day by a dedicated and inspiring team of employees and colleagues who became my family. I will be forever proud and grateful to each of them for all they created and accomplished.

Building the company also gave me the opportunity to travel across the country and to other continents, often with Jonny by my side. It gave me the finances and flexibility to enroll him in a private school, to take and pick him up each day, to chaperone his field trips, and to be there for the significant moments in his life. I even put a desk in my office where he did his homework after school each day. He was able to grow up with my employees treating him like a little brother.

As the company grew, so did we. My son grew into a man who exceeded all my dreams. He married his high school sweetheart. Together they have committed their lives to helping others and making this planet a better place.

Six years into building the company, I was blessed to meet a remarkable man, Mark. Mark had never been married but had a lifelong dream of having a family.

He pursued me, and we were married within a year. He stepped into our lives at just the right time. He adopted Jonny a couple of years into our marriage and supported him through the tough times and good times. He lives life as though his dream is to make sure we achieve our dreams. He is an amazing man who treats me like a queen.

DEVELOPING A
SIMPLICITY MINDSET

ONE OF MY FAVORITE QUOTES of all time is from Leonardo da Vinci, who said, "Simplicity is the ultimate sophistication." Da Vinci is known as one of the world's greatest scientists. But he was also an artist, architect, mathematician, and inventor. His words carry a lot of credibility and inspiration across the spectrum from art to science, even business.

But this quote is far more than just a quaint saying on a coffee mug or calendar. It's a message that encourages us to keep things simple. It's a principle that has inspired and empowered thousands of unlikely people to achieve extraordinary levels of success. It's a principle that has inspired me throughout my career.

The message of simplicity is at the very core of the AUDIT Principle. Certain concepts, if applied to your life or business, can completely transform you and launch you to higher levels of living. Simplicity is one of these concepts, and it's a key to understanding and applying the AUDIT Principle.

Whether it's raising operating capital to start a company, navigating the daily challenges of life, or just enjoying life more fully, the concept of simplicity has served to guide me through every stage of my personal, spiritual, and professional development. It can do the same for you.

Simplicity is the state or quality of being simple. Keeping things simple should always be a key objective, whether you are making choices, pursuing goals and dreams, designing or developing new products, or making new plans. Focusing on simplicity allows you to get started quickly and keeps the momentum moving forward toward your goals and dreams.

It's when things become complicated and complex that forward momentum begins to wane and progress tends to get bogged down. Eventually, you find yourself dead in the water, having completely lost your momentum.

But just because something is simple doesn't mean it's easy. Some of the simplest things can be the hardest to execute. And just because it's simple doesn't mean it's not powerful. Don't dismiss its power to transform.

Applying the principle of simplicity starts with developing and maintaining a "simplicity mindset." It's like a simplicity filter through which you process the world, the thoughts and ideas that pass through your mind. You make the decision to see the world through a different lens than most of the world.

This principle was illustrated to me one time while on vacation. My husband and I joined another couple on a charter boat in Mexico. We were lounging on the deck when the captain shouted to us that there was a whale shark next to the boat. Looking over the side, I immediately saw the huge shark.

When my husband and friends looked over the side of the boat, they couldn't see it. It was right there, alongside the boat, yet they couldn't see this magnificent creature. Then it dawned on me. I was wearing my "Maui Jim" sunglasses. I could see what the others couldn't because I was looking through polarized lenses.

Maui Jim's have a special polarized lens that enables you to see through the glare of the ocean's surface. One by one, they each had to put on my sunglasses in order to see the shark clearly. They were unable to see beyond the surface until they changed the lenses they were looking through.

We all have opportunities and dreams within our reach, but to see them become a reality, we need to be looking through the right set of lenses. We need to see our goals and dreams as attainable. We need to see them through a set of lenses that allows us to see ourselves as capable and qualified. Seeing through a lens of simplicity empowers you to see what others are unable to see and accomplish what others are unable to accomplish.

SIMPLICITY IS MORE EFFECTIVE

Simplicity as a mindset allows you to dream big. It's a child-like faith that believes that if others can be successful, you can be successful too. If your competitors can do it, you can do it, if others can be promoted, you can be promoted. If others can achieve their dreams, you can achieve your dreams. At its most basic level, the simplicity mindset sets the stage for us to adopt a can-do attitude.

The empowering thing about simplicity as a mindset is that it unlocks you and frees you to get started. The business and personal landscape is full of goals, dreams, and visions that have never seen the light of day all because they were never initiated. By keeping things simple, you're able to lower the threshold of beginning, making it easier to get out the gate. And once you're started, your courage and creativity will build like a fresh wind in your sails, creating forward momentum.

But be forewarned. Most people don't see things simply; they assume that the more complex it is, the more successful it can be. And they apply that assumption to business, thinking that in order to be successful, the business design has to be a complex one. However, the owners of successful companies have, in many cases, taken intentional steps to keep things simple. Warren Buffett, the billionaire businessman said, "The business schools reward difficult, complex behavior, but simple behavior is more effective."

Mr. Buffett isn't saying that education holds no value at all. Education is extremely valuable, and the more education you get, the more opportunities you'll be able to pursue. However, you should never let teachers, company assessments, or advisors tell you that you can't achieve something just because they don't believe. Just because you may have struggled in a particular subject at school, weren't very good at taking exams, or didn't get a college degree doesn't mean you aren't qualified to do something great.

There is a Presbyterian church in my old neighborhood with a marque where they post positive sayings. One day when I was struggling with my lack of qualifications and credentials for business, I happened to drive by the church. The marque proclaimed, "God doesn't call the qualified, He qualifies the called." That quote encouraged me and served to remind me to look through the right lens.

Over the years I've failed to score well on all kinds of tests, from academic to a multitude of corporate, personality and psychological assessments designed to measure my aptitude for success. Because of my dismal performance in high school, my college entrance counselor actually advised me to pursue the arts and stay away from some of the more academically challenging majors. Yet, in spite of the negative testing and my low ranking on many assessments, I've been able to build successful companies, train and lead hundreds of employees and volunteers, and continue to contribute positively within multiple organizations. I'm making a difference in my community in spite of what those tests indicated. I'm convinced that I've been able to succeed not because of my credentials or degrees, but because of my simplicity mindset, which has been fueled by faith.

TRANSFORM YOUR MINDSET

So how do you change your mindset? How do you shift to a simplicity mindset that will cause you to think and dream bigger? How do you expand your thinking so you can do more, be more, and achieve more?

We've all heard the saying, "Garbage in, garbage out." If you are putting garbage in your mind, then garbage is what you can expect your mind to produce. The things you listen to and watch, over time, are going to be the things you think about. And as you know, the things you think about are the things you'll end up doing.

That's why you should always make it a point to listen to positive, instructional, and motivational messages that will get your mind in the right place, developing a can-do attitude.

One of the worse things we can do is allow our thinking to become negative, because it's negative thinking that leads to a scarcity mindset. This is the mindset that tells you that there is only so much pie to go around. This is exactly the kind of destructive thinking that will undermine your efforts at every turn.

Positive thinking, on the other hand, leads to an abundance mindset, which stresses that there is plenty of goodness, resources, and opportunity to go around. Just because one person has more doesn't mean there's less for me. Switching from a scarcity mindset to an abundance mindset requires effort and repetition, just like transforming any other bad habit into a good one.

The great news is that with the Internet, we are blessed to live in a time when we have access to unlimited material to listen to or watch, literally 24/7. There is little you can't learn through the endless supply of YouTube videos, podcasts, books, seminars, church services, and online streaming.

A powerful technique for changing and developing your mindset is to create a daily discipline to feed your mind with good, healthy things. Think of it like eating. Most of us are disciplined to eat three meals a day. You can eat junk food, which makes you sluggish, or you can eat healthy food, which gives you energy. In both cases, you're feeding your body, but because of the type of food you choose, you achieve different results. Feeding your mind works the same way. When you feed your mind with good, positive input, it will generate positive energy and action.

My life is a testimony to this principle. Although I didn't have the benefit of a business degree, I developed a positive mindset, which led to the faith that I could start, build, and sell a company. This mindset was created in large part by attending conferences, building new relationships, and listening to thousands of hours of instructional and motivational tapes, CDs, and videos. It was in listening and applying those positive messages that I ultimately gained the inspiration, belief, and the faith to achieve what seemed impossible.

But success relies on more than just you and your positive outlook on life. You must have the faith to believe that others will come alongside at key moments of your journey and bring along the skills you will need at just the right time. Have faith that God, and the entire universe, are supporting and cheering you on.

There is one more key ingredient to your success that goes beyond a positive outlook or being surrounded by a supportive team. You have to be disciplined enough to step out and do the hard work that success requires. Success is about action and having the courage to take the bold steps forward.

Writing this book has been a whole new challenge for me. Throughout this process, it wasn't unusual to encounter brain block, causing me to be unable to get the right words on the page. When this happened, I stayed positive and reminded myself of what I have accomplished already. I told myself, "Jane Ann, you built a company from scratch, and nothing in your life has been harder than that. You wrote a business plan and thousands of letters to potential investors, clients, employees, and regulators, you designed marketing materials and waded through hundreds of bids, and you even created the acquisition book. For crying out loud, you got this!"

And you've got this too! You can do whatever you put your mind to as long as you believe. When you keep things positive by keeping things simple, you can accomplish your goals, dreams, and visions. But just like anything else, the simplicity mindset takes practice, and like any skill, it will need to be developed over time with lots of repetition and practice. So practice exercising your simplicity mindset. Not only will you attract new opportunities, you'll accelerate success and have more fun along the way!

Now that we have your mind in the right place, it's time to go through the AUDIT Principle step by step. These steps are important if you want to succeed and make it all the way to your destination.

A is for ASSESS. Before you begin, you must be able to accurately assess your address, your starting point.

U is for UNDERSTAND. Understand where you want to go and why.

D is for DECIDE. Once you know your starting point and you understand where you want to go and why, it's time to make several important decisions, including which vehicle is going to be the right one to get you there.

I is for IMAGINE. Now that you have decided upon the vehicle, it's time to imagine your plan. How are you going to get to your destination?

T is for SEEING IT THROUGH. Many people get started, but only the committed see things all the way through to the very end.

Now that you know what the letters stand for, it's time to fully explore them one at a time, starting with the letter A.

7

ASSESS YOUR ADDRESS

THE ELEMENTS of the AUDIT Principle were growing and developing under the radar all throughout my life, but it was really that first audit of my company that caused the principle to crystallize into a form I could grasp and, more importantly, share with others.

On that day, just before the Christmas holiday, when I heard those words from my brother and CFO, I knew an audit was serious business. And while I knew the process would be a challenging one, I knew it would be a positive thing, putting our company on a higher plain and allowing us to achieve even more than we thought possible.

Now more than a decade later and having participated in multiple audits, I've learned their value and benefits (as well as the costs and inconvenience). I've learned how to prepare, how to respond, and how to work with regulators, accounting firms, and others involved in each audit.

Every audit I've undergone has helped me grow and learn to function at a higher level of productivity. They have caused me to put needed systems in place and to identify and correct areas that needed attention. They have served to build my companies' reputation and have increased my confidence.

And the AUDIT Principle isn't just for business. Since the days of that first audit, I've discovered the principle works anytime you want to leave Point A and move to Point B, whether the project is losing weight, building a network of relationships, writing a book, or starting a company. Anytime you want to leave where you are and make your way to somewhere else, the AUDIT Principle will serve as a road map.

But even though we think, we dream, we plan, we strategize, we whiteboard and workshop ideas, we often don't know how to take that first step. We stutter and stammer and start to step out, but then we pull back. And the longer it takes us to move forward, the more our confidence slips. We lose momentum and, once again, the project or dream finds its way to the back burner.

The AUDIT Principle gets you off the mark with a checklist to get you where you want to go. But unlike a regulatory audit, the AUDIT Principle doesn't highlight or disqualify you just because of your mistakes or lack of qualifications. In fact, when we are weak in an area and follow the AUDIT Principle's steps, our weaknesses can become strengths, even accelerators in achieving our goal and arriving at our desired outcomes.

One more thing before we dive in. The AUDIT Principle is designed to use with projects that have movement built in, like moving from Point A to Point B. You're going to have to make a change of some kind. You can't keep on doing the same thing and expecting different results. When you're ready to take that bold step, that's where the AUDIT Principle helps out the most.

Okay, let's dive in!

A FOR "ASSESS"

The 5-step AUDIT Principle is based on the 5 letters of the word "A-U-D-I-T." The first step in the process is to "ASSESS YOUR ADDRESS." What I mean by that is you need to know where you are right now in relationship to where you want to be.

Where do you live, work, and function today, and does that align with your values, goals, and dreams? Do where you are and what you are doing align with the outcomes and destination you want to experience and achieve?

The purpose of an audit is to confirm that your business is legal and capable of doing what it was created to do. The audit looks at specific areas to confirm that each system, process, and regulatory requirement complies or aligns with the appropriate laws.

The AUDIT Principle works in the very same way. Assessing your address is simply the process of confirming that where you are and what you are doing complies with what YOU have been created to be and do. And if you determine that where you are and what you are doing today is not serving your values, goals, and dreams, then you may find yourself facing a defining moment. You will be challenged with the question, "Am I courageous enough to act on this new knowledge?"

So, the first thing you need to determine is your current location. Only then can you begin to chart a course to your destination. Remember, the map of store locations at the mall doesn't help much unless you can find the red X that tells you, "You are HERE."

There are three key elements to assessing your address:

- Assess your location
- Assess your values
- Assess your activities

ASSESS YOUR LOCATION: WHERE ARE YOU RIGHT NOW?

Does where you live, work, and spend time align with your values, goals and dreams? In real estate investing, there is well-known adage that states when you make a move or investment, your top three considerations should be location, location, location.

My parents have been a strong example for me as to the importance of assessing location. They lived out the principle of "location, location, location" in every decision they made.

My father and mother met on a blind date in Chicago. At the time, my dad was attending dental school and my mom was enrolled at the Chicago Art Institute. Upon graduating, my dad, as well as many of his classmates, was immediately drafted into the Navy. He spent two years aboard a ship serving as both the ship's dentist and doctor before returning to Chicago and my mom.

When his tour of duty was over, my dad went back to

school one final year to get his board certification as an orthodontist. Armed with his board certification, along with a few years of experience under his belt, he and my mom were ready to select the location to launch their new life together.

Rather than staying in Chicago or moving to another heavily populated city, my parents decided to launch my dad's practice and start their family in Fargo, North Dakota. Being a rural community with a low population, Fargo may seem like an unlikely destination for an ambitious graduate with big dreams.

However, Fargo was just their first step. It wasn't their ultimate destination to live and raise their family, but they understood the importance of location. They knew that Fargo was a place that would support their values while serving as the greatest "launching pad" to get where they wanted to be in the quickest way possible.

There were a few factors that they carefully considered as they assessed the Fargo location. First, my grandfather was a doctor who practiced in the nearby town of Morehead, Minnesota. Being a country doctor who made house calls, delivered babies, and saved lives meant my grandparents were well-known and loved all over the region. Moving to Fargo gave my father the immediate advantage of his parents' good name and reputation.

Second, there was only one orthodontist practicing in Fargo and the surrounding areas, and he wasn't board certified. My dad was able to launch and build his practice quickly without the competition that a city or region with a greater population would have. Many of my dad's patients drove hundreds of miles, from as far away as South Dakota, to receive treatment. By going where other graduates weren't willing to go, my dad experienced almost immediate success.

Finally, Fargo was a small town that supported my parents' values. It allowed them to be near family, buy a nice home, and become contributing members of the community, all while generating the resources necessary to fulfill their dream and move to their ultimate destination of California.

Although Fargo was home for a season and a place of abundance, for my parents it was a transitional or temporary stepping stone along their journey to achieving their dreams.

Assessing your location is more than researching and identifying weather patterns, safe neighborhoods, and good investments. There's more to consider when determining where to work, live, and spend time. It's important to view your locations as intermediate stepping stones and launching pads along the way toward achieving your ultimate destination.

ASSESS YOUR VALUES: WHAT'S IMPORTANT TO YOU?

The second element is to Assess Your Values. This is the step where you take an honest look at what's most important to you. What is it in your life that really matters? This assessment is by you, but it's not just for you. Your life, and the success you achieve, impacts the world around you and even beyond you. You have been created and placed on earth for a purpose that only you are able to fulfill. Whether your impact is gentle like a ripple in a pond or bold, exploding out like a sonic boom, your life touches others, and what you do with it is significant.

Assessing and identifying what's important to you gives you clarity and purpose. And as you move forward, it gives you the "why" behind the decisions you will be making.

Assessing your values doesn't need to be a long and difficult process, but it does require honesty and thoughtfulness. It requires that you identify what's important to you AND the lives you will be impacting. This is true whether the goal is realizing a business strategy or a life's dream.

An example of this would be if you were considering a new project in your business. You can either decide to outsource the project to an outside vendor, or you can choose to hire employees to get the same outcome. Your values will likely play a role in the decision you make, and your decision will most certainly affect others.

This is the exercise I followed as a seventeen-year-old student, right after my teacher wrote in my journal, "Jane Ann, I see you floating down a river without rudder or sail." Although my dream was to live a life of significance and to make a difference in the world, I didn't know what that meant or how to live it out.

But that day her comments motivated me to finally decide what I was going to do with my life. I raced home with a simple strategy: to identify the top values that my future career path would need to have and then pick a career path that met each of those values.

Across the top of a legal pad, I wrote, "What's Important to Me." I then proceeded by listing the five core values my chosen occupation would have to include.

The cool thing about this exercise is that although I didn't ultimately become a doctor, it led to me to creating and following a plan. In the process, opportunities presented themselves that better aligned with my values *and* my strengths.

"Identifying Your Values" is an important step in the assessment process because your values become an important metric in making your assessments and future decisions.

Assessing your values challenges you to decide if where you are and what you are doing complies with what you have been created to be and do. It challenges you to ask the question, "Does where I am and what I'm doing align with what's ultimately important to me and to those I serve? Does this lead to my ultimate destination?"

ASSESS YOUR ACTIVITIES: THE BARNACLE PRINCIPLE

The third component to assessing your address is the step of identifying whether your activities align with your values, goals, and dreams. As you honestly assess the way you spend your time, do you find that your habits support your values? Do you find that your relationships and commitments move you toward your desired destination, or do those things distract you from your ultimate goal?

We all have a limited amount of time on Planet Earth, which makes our time precious. Time is one of the greatest resources we possess. Knowing this, one of the most valuable things we can do is to look at how we are spending it. We do this by assessing our activities, highlighting what we are doing and who we are doing it with.

Are we working late most nights and missing dinner with

our family? Does business travel keep us away from attending our children's games and performances? Does our volunteer work or the hobbies we pursue exclude our family? Are our schedules so busy that we are too tired to exercise, eat well, spend time with family, or live the life we've dreamed of living?

Although you may be spending your time doing positive and worthwhile activities, if you don't routinely assess your activities, things can begin to slip. You can easily discover that you've allowed yourself to become too busy and distracted from what's most important to you. I call this the Barnacle Principle, because like barnacles growing on the bottom of a boat, our activities can be growing faster than we realize. As a sailor I've been reminded of this lesson more than once!

When you sail, you can't just aim in the direction you want to go. You are not able to simply turn right or left to get to your destination. The reason? You are subject to the laws of sailing. You must adjust your sail to align with the direction of the wind.

For example, if the wind is behind you, you "run" with the wind, filling your sail. If the wind is coming at an angle, you must "tack" back and forth in order to get to your ultimate destination.

When you don't align your sails to the wind, there are a couple of likely consequences. If the sail is unable to properly fill with the wind, you will probably become stuck, known as being "caught in irons." The sail simply flaps in the wind. On the other hand, if the sail fills with the wind too quickly and is pulled too taut, you may inadvertently capsize the boat.

But there's a third culprit that can keep you from getting where you want to go when you sail. And it's something they didn't teach in my sailing class. I discovered this during my first year of college when my brother and I leased a 25-foot sailboat. I'll never forget the first time I took several of my coworkers out for an excursion on this boat.

I hadn't gone far before discovering that something was very wrong. I properly tacked with the wind, but when we tried to turn, the boat began to drift. The only workable corrective action was to quickly turn on the engine and motor through each turn. No matter what I tried, with each attempted turn, the boat seemed intent on going its own way. After several embarrassing attempts, I was forced to motor the boat back to its dock.

I discovered later that the bottom of the boat was covered with barnacles. The owner had failed to clean the hull before leasing it to us. As a result, each time I attempted to negotiate a turn, the weight of the barnacles forced the boat to drift the opposite direction. There was no way the boat could sail to its destination until the barnacles were removed.

Volumes have been written regarding the parallels between life and sailing. For example, it's easy to get "caught in irons" for failing to align our sails with what the wind is doing. We can even capsize the boat if we don't follow the appropriate laws of the wind.

My experience with the barnacles proved to be one of the most significant lessons yet. Many have to learn this lesson by embarrassing and sometimes painful experience. It's a lesson seldom taught and too often caught.

Barnacles include the negative "time thieves" like bad habits, poor processes, and unhealthy relationships. But barnacles can also be good activities like volunteer work, committee assignments, and working overtime.

When you take a careful look at these things, you might realize right now might not be the best time to be doing some of the activities you are trying to fit in, even if they're good. Although many of your activities may be positive and bringing you a level of pride and contribution, the timing may be off. If not removed from your schedule, they can distract, delay, or even derail you from arriving at your desired destination.

Find yourself drifting? Check for barnacles!

As you pursue your goals, dreams, and visions, consider the following strategy: periodically conduct an examination to make sure you are purging the barnacles that attach themselves to you and your organization. Assess your activities to determine whether or not they align with your values, goals, and dreams. Think of this practice as the "Barnacle Principle."

Assessing your activities and then eliminating the ones that aren't in alignment will help get you to your destination in the quickest way possible. If you eliminate the unnecessary things, it frees you up to focus on what's necessary.

A DANGEROUS STEP

We've talked about the three key elements in assessing your address. But before we end the chapter, I want to warn you about a particularly dangerous tendency we can all fall prey to.

When we are assessing our address, we can be tempted to shift our focus onto other people and the journeys that they are on instead of keeping our focus on our own journey. This is the dangerous step of comparing ourselves with others.

Each of us are unique individuals. And each of us have been created with a unique purpose greater than we have the capability or the proper perspective to fully understand. If we keep our vision and focus on where we are and where we are going, we will be able to experience more than we could ever imagine.

On the other hand, if we allow our focus to shift off our own journey and onto that of someone else's, we can run into real problems. Comparing yourself to someone else can cause confusion, derailing you from fulfilling a destiny that's uniquely yours. This tendency to compare can keep you from making a difference that's all your own.

Remember, to make a difference, you need to BE different. This is YOUR adventure, and it won't look like anyone else's. Certainly, you should be encouraged by other people's successes and learn from other people's mistakes, but you should never compare yourself with someone else.

Now that you've assessed your address, it's time for you to take the next step in the AUDIT Principle.

8

UNDERSTAND YOUR DESTINATION

Now that you have **Assessed** your address and have a good feel of your starting point, it's time to move on to the next step of the AUDIT Principle. Before you can make a plan, determine your objectives, estimate a timeline, or establish a budget, you have to be very clear on where you're heading. You have to **Understand Your Destination**.

What is your dream? What do you want to achieve? Who do you want to become? What difference do you want to make? The answers to these questions will determine your desired destination.

Being committed to understanding and reaching your destination is key to living an empowered life because it requires that you live intentionally, to actually identify where you want to end up. You are no longer wandering through life aimlessly. You are intentionally taking positive steps today because you know that they are the key to being in the right place tomorrow. When the destination has been defined, every step you take has a reason and an objective.

Do you have any idea how rare that is today? There are those who may have dreams of living in a bigger house or driving a nicer car, but that's about as specific as their dream gets. General dreams do not lead to specific outcomes. When you are able to define your destination clearly, you immediately set yourself apart from a majority of the crowd.

Your destination, and your understanding of it, becomes your metric for almost every decision you'll make along your journey. Even more importantly, the destination will determine the choices you'll make along the way.

VACATION DESTINATION

When it's time for a vacation, you identify why you want to take the vacation in the first place before you choose a destination. Before you can know the "where," you have to identify the "why."

Do you want to relax on a beach or learn a new language? Do you want to explore a new culture or surround yourself with what's familiar? Do you want to attend a conference with hundreds of others or go on a solo adventure?

Each of these "whys" will determine a very different and specific "where."

Knowing your destination allows you to identify the vehicles, resources, time, and relationships you're going to need to get there. For example, if you are in New York and you want to plan a trip to Los Angeles, you have several choices as to what vehicle to choose. You can take a plane or a car. If you're ambitious, you might even bike. I suppose you could consider taking a cruise ship as well if you wanted to take the long way around.

If your desire is to have a vacation of adventure or to lose weight, then maybe the vehicle you choose would be the bicycle. Or if you want to explore other cultures, then maybe the ocean voyage taking you through the Panama Canal would be the right choice to make. In these cases, you're acknowledging that the journey itself is as important as getting to the destination.

On the other hand, if you really need to get to LA quickly, you'll want to opt for the plane, maybe even a charter. With this choice, you're determining that getting to the coast quickly is your top priority. Your defined purpose of going to LA has a direct bearing on the vehicle you choose. This shows just how important the purpose is to the overall decision-making process.

All of these are viable options depending on how much you want to spend and how long you want the journey to take. The fact that the trip is a long one and all the way across the country helps define and narrow down your vehicle options.

But let's say your destination changes. Now you want to go to Hawaii instead of Los Angeles. This new destination gives you different parameters to consider. Because of the ocean you'll have to cross, the option of taking a car is no longer on the table and neither is the bike. By understanding that your destination is in the middle of the Pacific Ocean, you're able to make informed decisions about the vehicle you should choose.

There's no shortage of businesses that fail, marriages that

result in divorces, and dreams that go unfulfilled because those involved didn't take the time to assess their starting place and understand where they wanted to go and why.

Let me give you a personal example. Early in my career, I assumed that success was mostly about one thing: the destination. I thought once I made it rich, I could join the country club and meet people of influence. And once I was able to do those things, the right doors would open for me.

But it was in walking out the dream on a daily basis, navigating the various challenges, responding to opposition, managing employees, working with vendors, and responding to legal and regulatory road blocks that I really began to build the relationships I needed in order to develop influence.

The real value of my journey was not in arriving at the destination and "striking it rich." All the little things that, when combined, became the fulfillment of my dream. While arriving at my goal gave me a certain level of wealth and credibility, the real value was hammered out along the way. The destination is the goal that points us in the right direction, provoking us to do the right things for the right reasons.

DEFINING THE DESTINATION

How do you break down the process of understanding your destination? As I pointed out earlier, you begin by asking yourself a lot of very pointed, very honest questions. It's the answers you come up with that will help shape your destination.

When my husband David died, I was thrust into a role I was ill-prepared for. My world shifted when I suddenly became my son's sole provider. The questions and strategies that David and I had addressed early on as a young couple for raising and providing for our son had to be figured out all over again. No longer was there a "we." Now it was just "me." Now there were new realities in my world that I had to take into consideration.

As I wrestled with the questions and challenges that most single parents face, a new and different destination for my life emerged that evolved around my son.

THE WRONG VEHICLE

Through this process of asking questions, I could see that I needed to free up more time in my day to spend with Jonny. Having the time to pour into my son became my new destination. The problem was finding more time. I had been given promotions at work, which was nice, but the changes caused a dilemma for me.

It's always flattering to be considered for promotions and raises. One way to view the increased responsibilities and compensation is as an open door. I could have thought, *Positive things are happening as I travel down this road. I should keep moving in this direction. This has to be the right way.*

But fortunately, I was keenly aware that along with those promotions came a high cost. My job was demanding more travel, and that took more and more time away from Jonny, time that was valuable to me. Instead of freeing up more time for Jonny, I was actually spending more time away from him. I was moving in a direction I didn't want to go. In this new light, I could see that I was no longer willing to pay the higher price that came with the promotions and increased salary.

My job had provided me with a great life in the past, but my circumstances had changed. And those changes meant a change in destinations. With the new destination defined, it was time to choose a different vehicle to get me where I wanted to go.

As long as your vehicle is moving you toward your goals and dreams, the vehicle is serving its purpose. However, if you find that the vehicle is no longer taking you toward your desired future, it is time to reassess. Just like the vacation example. When your destination changes from Los Angeles to Hawaii, your vehicle will need to change.

EVALUATE YOUR PRIORITIES

It's this kind of honest assessment of where you are and where you want to go that allows you to evaluate your priorities. What's important to you? Are you actively pursuing those things or hoping that they will just magically appear while you're on your way to your destination in pursuit of other things? The truth is that the things we pursue in life are usually the only things we actually obtain.

Over time, if we are not careful, we tend to get a little distracted concerning our priorities. We subtly shift along the way, and although we still maintain that we treasure values like time with family, romance, pursuing a healthy lifestyle, or travel with those we love, one look at our calendar or our checkbook, and the truth says otherwise. We're not actually pursuing the things we say we are.

We lose our way and forget that the career we chose was going to serve us, not the other way around. We wake up one day to find that we're spending nearly all our time not with our family but with our coworkers. We're giving them our best time and nearly all our energy. We arrive home at the end of each day too exhausted to spend much quality time with those we love the most, and yet we say that they're the ones we're working so hard for.

Sadly, there are many men and women who start their own company with the very best of intentions. They want to have the flexibility of time along with the eventual promise of financial independence. But instead they find themselves working much harder than they used to, spending way more time doing tasks they don't enjoy. Understanding this process leads to the realization that their vehicle isn't taking them where they want to go.

The process of working through this helped me understand that my job wasn't my identity. It didn't define who I was. I had gained the clear understanding that my job was simply a vehicle that would help me get to my ultimate destination, and it was no longer supporting my needs, goals, or dreams.

This was a new thought for me, and it was hard to wrap my head around at first. I had begun working for the company as the receptionist in a little office in Irvine, California, at the age of twenty-two. This company opened up new vistas for me, taking me across the country and introducing me to an entire industry. This was the company I had grown up with, allowing me to hone new skills and build relationships while developing confidence along the way. I had even begun to build a reputation within the industry as a woman who worked hard and could get things done. I loved what I did and was good at it.

Yet in spite of all of the benefits and promises of new opportunities ahead, my situation had changed, and I was no longer the person I once had been. My priorities had undergone a shift. Now, I wanted to be there for my son. I wanted to live the kind of life that showed we can be whoever we want to be. I wanted to live out the example that we could make a difference with our lives and with our finances.

In the process of hammering out an understanding of my new destination, I became aware of a new decision I would have to make. If my current job was the wrong vehicle, then what would be the right vehicle? What vehicle was going to support my goals, dreams, and visions now that my life situation had changed? I had to plan for a whole new future, one that looked very different than the one I had planned with David.

To see your destination clearly, you have to take a step back, remove emotion from the equation, and take a hard look at where you want to go. No excuses. No denial, just an honest evaluation.

In the last chapter we spent a great deal of time talking about assessing your current address, taking an honest look at where you are right now as you begin your journey. Now I'm talking to you about taking your eyes off your feet and casting your vision to the horizon. Before you can travel anywhere successfully, you need a complete understanding of your destination.

DESCRIBING THE DESTINATION TO OTHERS

But understanding our destination isn't just for us. Understanding where we want to go will help us recruit others to join us in our quest. The fact is, no matter who we are or how many resources we may have at our disposal, we're going to need the help of others to be successful. No one can accomplish what they need all on their own. If you can accomplish your dream all by yourself, your dream isn't big enough.

We need to understand our destination, our vision, and dream well enough to explain it to others. At first, your dream destination might be a little fuzzy or lack definition. And while that might be okay for you, unless there's more definition, you'll never be able to explain it in a way that will make sense to others. And if they don't catch your vision, they'll never be able to rally around and support it.

That's why this step is so vitally important. If you've got a muddled, unclear vision, then others are never going to be able to latch on to what you're trying to do. Somewhere along the way, we all need the help, the resources, the financial assistance, or the encouragement of someone else. And if they're going to come along side to help, you're going to have to have more than a fuzzy idea of where you want to go.

Let's say you want to build your dream home. Very few of us have the skill at all the various steps of construction to actually build our own dream home. Even the most talented builders will often bring in experts to do things they don't know how to do as well.

As long as the dream home is merely a picture in your mind, it'll never become a reality. Before others can grab it, it has to become accessible. It has to get out of your mind. You have to open up and put words to your dream so you can share it with others. Words are like handles that give your dreams something others can grab onto.

When we're able to describe our dream in detail, then the architect can draw it. Once it's drawn, the builder will be able to make his blueprints. From that point, the plan is able to come together with a timeline, a materials list, and a budget. So the process starts with your dream, then you bring the dream to life using words so others can come alongside you to help.

SHARING MY OWN DREAM

When I stepped out to start my own company, I knew there was no way I could do it all on my own. I needed money, so after creating a detailed and compelling business plan, I set about to raise the capital. As my plan began to take shape, excitement and momentum grew. I was eager to share my new vision with others.

Armed with a cup of hot tea and a list of phone numbers of potential investors, I began making calls. Day after day I called the names on my list, eagerly pitching the benefits of investing in my company. Although everyone was kind and offered up helpful words of encouragement, no one chose to invest. I had some great conversations with a lot of nice people, but I had no more money after calling all the folks on my list than what I'd started out with. To say I was discouraged is an understatement. I felt utterly defeated.

Then a family friend shared a story I'd never heard before. It was a story about my father. He told me about how, years earlier, my father invited him to invest in a building project he was planning. After patiently listening to my father's pitch, the friend declined the offer to invest.

Then, a few days later, my father unexpectedly showed up on this friend's doorstep with two plane tickets in his hand. He held them out and said, "Hurry and pack your suitcase, we're going to New York to meet with a banker!" It amazes me to this day, but somehow, my father was able to talk his friend into an impromptu cross-country flight.

During their long flight, my father had his friend right where he wanted him, trapped in the seat next to him. Flying at 30,000 feet, my father was able to inspire this man to cosign on a loan which would provide the funding necessary for the building. It proved to be a very good investment for both of them.

After hearing this story, it occurred to me that the only difference between the offer that got turned down and the offer that was accepted was a change in my father's strategy. His old strategy was to ask people for money to help him build a building. But the new strategy (apart from trapping him on a plane!) was to cast a vision about an exciting project he wanted his friends to join.

His new strategy involved a shift in perspective. Instead of asking people to give him money, he was including people in his vision. And somewhere in the sky between Southern California and New York City, our family friend caught the vision.

His story inspired me to change my own funding strategy. That day I decided to quit asking people to invest in my company and simply begin to communicate my vision with each potential investor. I shared that, together, we were going to build a company and sell it for a profit. I explained that not only would the vision be a great investment, but it would also create hundreds of jobs and support causes we were all passionate about. I closed most conversations with, "This new company will be a vehicle that will help each of us to achieve our goals, dreams, and visions."

The more I shared what we were going to achieve and become, the more others were able to catch the vision. Over the phone I was able to subtly shift the conversation from "my vision" to "our vision." It was the fact that I clearly understood my destination that allowed me to clearly communicate it to others.

As a result, the people I shared with began to catch the vision. Within days, prospective investors began calling me. The word was out: "Jane Ann has a vision worth listening to." Early on, most of my investors were friends, former employees, and colleagues. But as the months went by, momentum began to build. And my message became more refined. I became confident enough to pitch my vision to folks I met simply while in the course of living life. For example, I met one investor while visiting a friend in the hospital, another at a funeral, and another while making copies at Kinko's.

"A" is assessing your address and honestly evaluating your starting point. "U" is understanding your destination, where you want to go, and why you want to go there.

Now that we have our starting point and our destination established and evaluated, we have a ready reference point for direction and encouragement. We're able to decide on the best, most efficient vehicle to get us there.

Like the North Star has been to sailors for countless years, understanding our destination allows us to not only start off on the right foot, it enables us to stay on course during the challenging moments of our journey.

Now for the next step. It's time to Decide!

9

DECIDE

O NCE YOU'VE **Assessed** your address and you **Under-stand** where you want to go, it's time to make a few important **Decisions**. Being able to make strong decisions is key for your success in any venture. Those who have trouble making decisions will have trouble moving forward.

DECIDE TO GO FOR IT

The first decision you need to make is that you're really going to do this. And you're going to go all the way. You're not just going to start, you're going to finish. This is the time when you make the decision that you really are going to put in all the effort it will take in order to reach your destination regardless of your past, regardless of what the naysayers may be saying to you, and regardless of your perceived limitations. In short, this is the step where you decide that you are going to continue to put in the effort in spite of the obstacles looming ahead in your path.

In many ways, this step could be the most important one because it triggers forward movement on your part. Deciding to go for it is no easy thing. It's more than just a simple mental assent that a change needs to happen. You've assessed your address and you've identified that where you are today doesn't line up with your goal or desired destination. With this fresh understanding, you're now making the decision to pursue a new and definitive destination.

This intentional decision is packed full of purpose. And it's your sense of purpose that will empower you to get to your destination and not give up along the way.

And you will be tempted to give up. You will face obstacles in your venture. Let me say that again. You will face obstacles in your venture. Guaranteed. And in those difficult times, you're going to have to be rock-solid in your determination to work through them. That's what going for it is all about. And the strength of your determination will depend on the strength of your decision to go for it.

This decision is critical to your overall success. If you are on the fence about whether or not you're going to pursue this dream, or you're taking the attitude that you'll take a few steps and "see how it goes," you're destined to fail. If we give ourselves a way out, most of us will take it at the first sign of difficulty or hardship.

But don't get discouraged. Everyone makes mistakes. And you will grow as you continue to move forward because it is in navigating the challenges and hurdles that develops strong skills, builds confidence, creates new relationships, and establishes your reputation. Living life fully is an adventure, and as with every adventure, there will be the unexpected. So, expect the unexpected!

OPPOSITION FROM FRIENDS AND FAMILY

A common yet disappointing occurrence that often happens early into the process of pursuing our dreams is the discovery that there are lots of folks that don't share our excitement, faith, or optimism. What makes this doubly discouraging is that many times, these folks are our closest friends and family, the people who love us most.

This is true in every arena of life, whether it's in your work place, church, or family. Anytime we step out in faith to pursue a dream, we'd like it if we were cheered on from the sidelines and celebrated for our courage. We want to be able to share these exciting new opportunities with those we love. But you should know in advance that there will always be people who don't see your decision as a positive or even possible thing. Making the decision to go for it can be a very lonely proposition.

This is true at every stage in the pursuit of your goals and dreams. Sometimes it will seem as if you can't take a step without being challenged. Obstacles will rise up in the most unexpected places and times. Your decision to actually go for your dreams will be challenged time and time again. That's why getting a clear understanding of your purpose and your destination is so important.

For example, let's say you're a business owner or the manager of a growing company. One day, you realize that not all your employees are fully on board with the dream you have for the future of the company. Some don't have the ability to grow with you. Some don't even want the company to grow, they'd rather things stay just as they are. This can be challenging, even heartbreaking, especially when your team all started out on the dream together.

It's painful to realize that while you were busy celebrating each success, each step of forward progress, there were always some who dragged their feet, wanting to hang on to the status quo. They didn't want to see changes come to the company culture or to the processes they worked so hard to establish.

That's when you must stand strong. Not everyone will agree with your decision. Making the decision to go for it is deciding to change despite what others, even those who have been with you from the start, may say or think.

Whether it was my college counselor telling me I wasn't qualified to pursue my dream or family members telling me not to leave the security of my job or employees and colleagues wanting to maintain the status quo, I had many moments when I had to find the resolve to overcome discouragement. It was difficult to receive resistance from people I never expected to be so negative.

BE SELECTIVE WHEN YOU SHARE

Whether it's in pursuing dreams or in facing big challenges, it's always wise to be selective to whom we share our dream. For example, when I was diagnosed with breast cancer, I was careful about who I told.

I was determined to beat cancer, and I needed lots of encouragement in my battle. I had learned years earlier during David's courageous fight that people want to tell their own stories about loved ones who died after being diagnosed with similar cancers.

Listening to their negative stories right before going into my own battle was like being told in advance there was no hope and I shouldn't even bother fighting. All of us need hope and purpose to maintain our resolve. Our faith is built and made strong by the positive things we listen to and take to heart. It's this hope that keeps us going for our dream.

With this in mind, I made the decision that my brother would be the first person I called after receiving my diagnosis. Without hesitation, the first words out of Bob's mouth were, "Jane Ann, our friend Eileen had breast cancer and part of the reconstructive treatment is that you get a tummy tuck! You get your very own plastic surgeon and you don't even have to pay for it!"

My brother made me laugh, and we began creating stories about how after we sold my company I would be able to hang out with other successful women and compare our favorite "plastic surgeon" stories. Those few words encouraged me and gave me a vision of a successful outcome. Our conversations always made me laugh, all the way through recovery.

Throughout the process of writing this book, I've been reminded to be especially selective in who to share this dream with. It seems most everyone knows someone who has written a book or tried to write a book. At the end of the conversation, invariably the closing comment is, "No one ever makes money writing a book."

First of all, that's not true. Plenty of authors make money on the books they write. Statistically, it may be true that the majority of people don't make money; however, I've learned that statistics are just numbers. And I can empower them to either encourage me or discourage me. When you make the bold decision to go for it, you'll be able to defy the statistics.

It's a little like growing a plant from a seed. While the seed is young and still growing roots, we keep the plant protected in a greenhouse, away from the harmful elements like the hot sun or freezing temperatures. But once the seed has established roots, we are able to move the plant out of the greenhouse and plant it outside, where resistance can play its valuable role in the development and growth of the young plant.

The same is true in my case. Once I have roots established, each challenge, obstacle or opposition doesn't harm me or set me back but rather serves to build me up in ways that no college class or book can.

If you have goals and dreams stirring inside you and you don't know how to make them a reality, start by looking around you. Every business, every building, every venture or enterprise was started by someone just like you. Be encouraged by other people's successes, knowing that "if others can do it, you can do it." Then decide to go for it!

DECIDE TO DELETE

The next decision you're going to have to make is the decision to delete a few things from your process that will only serve to trip you up, delay your progress, or stop your venture altogether.

The first thing you must delete is your emotions. Your emotions go up and down, changing every day, sometimes multiple times each day. When you allow your emotions to rule, you are destined for a wild roller coaster ride.

One moment you'll be up on top of the world, thinking you can conquer anything. You feel like Superman or Wonder Woman and no matter what comes against you, you're confident that you will prevail.

The next thing you know, you get an email or a phone call with some bad news. Immediately your emotions fall and so does your mood. You feel defeated and all the wind is sucked out of your sails. Your forward progress grinds to a halt, and all your momentum is lost.

The funny thing about emotions is that they can soar or crater depending on the silliest things. Your favorite song comes on the radio and your emotions go through the roof. But let a song come on that reminds you of a bad memory, and your emotions drop through the floor. Songs, movies, food, even conversations can cause emotions to rise and fall. Your feelings are fickle and shouldn't be trusted. Delete your emotions from the decision-making process!

When David died, I went through a phase where I knew that my emotions should not be trusted. Because of the grief, my emotions were unreliable. I made the commitment to set my emotions aside for a season, believing there would be a time that my emotions would be healthy again.

In order to do this, it helped me to picture myself taking off a backpack. I imagined that this backpack was full of my emotions. I would visualize myself taking off the backpack and leaning it up against the wall or putting it in a closet out of sight. I was able to set aside my emotions until they were healthy enough to trust. Because I had determined my destination and understood my purpose, I was able to decide to delete my emotions and continue moving forward.

The next thing you need to delete are excuses. When we were kids, we'd try to get away with not turning in a homework assignment by telling the teacher that our dog ate our assignment. That excuse didn't work then, and your excuses as to why you can't complete your goal won't work now.

There are always a myriad of reasons why we should probably think twice before pursuing a venture. Maybe we think we're too old or too young, maybe we think we're not smart enough, don't have the right network, live in the wrong part of the country, don't drive the right kind of car, didn't go to the right college, and the list goes on ad nauseam.

It's not as if our excuses aren't true. In many cases they are true and valid, but that's not the point. If anyone had a long list of excuses as to why they shouldn't pursue something, it was me! I was a widowed single parent, with very few resources and no financial degree who wanted to start a highly regulated financial institution. On paper, there was no way I should've succeeded.

But the key to my success has never been about the finances or my education. The key to my success has always been that I was very clear about what my goal was. I understood what my desired destination was. Then I was able to follow the correct strategies, choosing the right vehicle to get where I wanted to go. Then I made the important and intentional decision to go for it. Failure was not an option. Emotions and excuses were replaced with faith and purpose.

The third thing you're going to have to delete from your decision-making process is fear. Fear paralyzes. And that's exactly what you don't want as you begin any venture. You don't want to be stuck in Park when you need to be in Drive.

Fear is an emotion that comes over us whenever we feel like we're in some kind of danger. That's true whether the danger is real or imagined. The ironic thing is that many times our fears don't cause us to move; they cause us to freeze in our tracks. It's like the nightmare we've all had when we're threatened by the monster but can't seem to get our legs to work. We're frozen in place.

It's the same way when we consider a challenging goal. We allow all the scary "what ifs" to paralyze us. We get our minds full of all kinds of doomsday scenarios and then imagine what we'll do if those things really come to pass. If you spend enough time thinking about all those things, you'll never even get started.

The most common fear, of course, is the fear of failure. We allow this fear to grow out of proportion into this massive thing. *What will happen if I fail? What will people think about me? I'll be labeled a failure and never be able to launch anything again!* Ultimately, we give those imaginations enough power to cause us to stop in our tracks. We seize up and fail to even take the first step.

Any venture we take forward into the future will take us into uncharted waters, where everything, every step is an unknown.

SURROUNDED BY SUPPORT

That's why I surrounded myself with people I could count on to bring me the wisdom and knowledge I needed to move forward. In my case, I found their presence in my life actually dispelled the fear. When these people were around, I was much more inclined to have the courage I needed to move forward, taking the steps I needed to take. My fear was tempered in their presence.

An adventure by yourself is seldom fun. However, when others are with you, the whole experience changes. When I'm sailing all by myself and a storm blows in, I get really frightened. The wind, the waves, the dark clouds closing in . . . it can be pretty scary.

But I can be in the same boat, with the very same storm heading my way, and if there are people in the boat with me, instead of getting frightened, the opposite occurs. I get bold. I might even show off a little!

This sense of confidence comes when others are in the boat with you. And why are you more confident? Because you're no longer alone. You're no longer relying on just your skills. Now you can take advantage of the skills and experience of everyone else in the boat with you. That's when your ordeal becomes an adventure and you become the author of your own adventure narrative, your own story.

Although I had the vision to start my company, I didn't feel like I had the skills to tackle it alone. I decided to approach potential partners. The people I recruited brought their own set of skills to make up for the ones I didn't have.

One of my partners was a dentist with a myriad of business experience that included an expertise in insurance. Another was a former colleague that had business operations experience. And one was my brother, who had the business finance experience. I asked each man, if I wrote the business plan and raised the money, would they join me? Each of them did.

There were benefits and challenges to having partners. But these benefits and challenges taught me important lessons. One lesson is while it is important to surround yourself with others (employees, partners, mentors, advisors, etc.), never forget this is your dream. And at the end of the day, you are ultimately the one to bring that dream to fruition.

The next thing you have to delete are the myths you've chosen to believe. An example of a myth that we've all believed at one time or another is, "I can't do this because no one has ever done it before." The myth that it can't happen because it's never happened before is not true. Don't eat before swimming, toads cause warts, and lightning never strikes in the same place twice are examples of myths we've all believed at one time or another.

But just because a myth isn't true doesn't make it less powerful. Down through history, myths, and people's beliefs in them, have altered the course of history. Myths have the power to shape your history too if you believe in them. In order to succeed in your venture, you'll have to determine which myths you are believing in and then make the decision to delete those myths from your thinking.

The last thing on my list of things you'll need to delete are the statistics or odds that say you'll never make it. Statistics are only statements about what has happened in the past. Successes are happening every day that defy the statistics. The odds were stacked against my success, but I'm living proof that you can defy those odds and succeed regardless of what the statistics say.

DECIDE WHICH VEHICLE

Now that you've made the decision to go for it and you've made your deletions, you're ready to decide which vehicle will best get you where you want to go. If you were to go car shopping today, you'd probably first think about what kind of car you need. Our choice of vehicle depends on what we need a vehicle to do for us and where we want that vehicle to take us. We need a vehicle that will support our purpose.

Like I mentioned before, if your destination is Hawaii, your best choice of vehicle would not be a car! Even if that car is the fastest, most expensive or most luxurious on the market, it will not get you across the Pacific Ocean to Hawaii.

Because of the influence and example of my parents, I was blessed to have a general idea of what I wanted my future to look like. They showed me that life is an adventure. They taught me the importance of education, family, success, and contribution.

But having a destination alone is not enough to make a quality decision on which vehicle might be the right one. To make that decision, you also need to be crystal clear on what is important in your ultimate destination and in the journey along the way. You must determine what values must be a part of every step of your life. These are your "Non-negotiables."

Going through the process of accessing what is important to you and creating a list of non-negotiables will empower you to select the best vehicle for getting to your destination. As a high school senior, I chose becoming a surgeon as my vehicle. But as I grew and discovered my strengths and talents, I picked a different vehicle.

I used the same process decades later when I decided to start my own company. I knew what my desired destination was. My destination was to give my son a happy childhood and future and show him life holds no limits. I wanted to travel to unique locations and make a positive difference in other people's lives. I chose an insurance company as my vehicle to do this.

I suppose I could've fallen in love with the idea of starting a coffee shop or a flower store or a marketing consulting business. But I didn't have the experience or the expertise in those areas. Also, these options would not afford me the lifestyle I desired. Those vehicles are wonderful for other people, but they didn't tick off the boxes on my list. In the end, I determined that an insurance company would allow me to do all the things on my list.

Years later, after selling my insurance companies, it was time to select a new vehicle that would continue to support my dream. I wanted to continue to live a life of making a difference, going places few people go, and reaching lives that are hard to reach.

How could I share my story in a way to help others? What would be the most effective way to share that life can be lived with few limits? In this new chapter in my life, what would my new vehicle need to be? I made the decision to write this book and take advantage of opportunities to speak publicly, telling my story and sharing the AUDIT Principle to all who will listen.

Your vehicle is the thing that will get you to your destination, whether that destination is a career goal, a financial goal, a weight loss goal, a creative goal, or a relationship goal.

Once you Decide, you're ready to Imagine!

IMAGINE

B Y THIS POINT IN THE PROCESS, you've **Assessed** your current address, you've come to the place where you **Understand** your destination, and you've made some critical **Decisions**, including what vehicle will best get you where you want to go.

Now it's time to **Imagine** and create your **plan**!

THE IMPORTANCE OF A PLAN

Almost no one makes an adequate plan. They don't take the time up front to imagine all the nuts and bolts they will need all along the way to accomplish their dream. They are anxious to get started, which is important, but it's foolish to launch off into almost any project without a good plan in place first.

Just like the process of writing this book. I would have never begun a venture like this without a plan. I didn't just go to my publisher and tell him I wanted to write a book. No, I had a plan. My idea for the book was developed, and I knew what I wanted to say. To further help me refine and focus my thoughts about the book, my publisher asked me a whole list of questions. Who was I writing to? What questions did I want the material to answer? What problems did I want to solve?

The answers to these questions helped the plan for the book take shape. Those questions helped me make an outline so I would know where I wanted to start and where I wanted to go with the content. In the same way, you should never start a business without a plan or start off on an adventure without consulting a map.

If you have a week-long vacation in front of you, your first step is to plan. You want to determine how much time and money you have to spend. Will you need to allow extra time for travel to a destination far away? If you spend all your time just getting to your destination, maybe you'll have to skip some of the side trips. You also want to determine what clothes you'll need to pack. What plans do you need to make for your house and your pets while you're away? With no plan, many of these important decisions will be overlooked.

Your destination will be different than mine, but the principle still holds true. I wanted to start a company because I wanted to be more in charge of my own time. I wanted to have financial independence and to experience life more fully. And I wanted to be there at the critical points of my son's life.

You have your own important decisions to make in this process. What's your destination? Where do you want to be? Do you want to be an entrepreneur? Do you want to build a business? What kind of vehicle will you need to get to your destination? Use your imagination to map out the answers to these questions. Decide what vehicle and path will take you where you dream of going. Go ahead, get excited!

AN IMPORTANT DISTINCTION

Remember, it's your vehicle that gets you to your destination. And it's your destination that will determine what type of vehicle you need, whether it's a car, bike, or airplane. In the AUDIT Principle, your vehicle is the project, venture, job, or decision that you choose to get you to your destination. And your destination represents your goal or dream.

It's important to understand this basic difference and not to confuse the two things. The reason is that as we live out our life, there's a tendency to get distracted and to let go of our actual goal or dream. We lose sight of where we want to go, who we want to become, and what we want to accomplish. We forget that the job, career, or venture we started is not our end goal; it's not our destination. It's only the vehicle that will get us to our destination.

This is why your plan is so important. Your plan is the big picture, where you are going and how you are going to get there. It's your plan that keeps you focused on the important things needed to get you to your ultimate destination. It becomes a blueprint or map that you and others can follow to build your vehicle, the one that will take you to your destination, the one that will take you to your goal, objective, or dream.

It is common to become so consumed with the process of building a vehicle that we mistakenly think the vehicle is the ultimate destination. It is an easy mistake to make when you are so invested in the process and surrounded by great people you enjoy working with.

But because I had a plan, I was able to stay focused on the target. My plan had a definite starting point and a clear finish line. I included our budget, timeline, and the commitment to our shareholders. It was the plan that guided our decisions over the years and helped them to remain aligned with our corporate goals and objectives. It was the plan that kept me accountable to the shareholders, to my son, and to the dreams we shared.

THE PLANNING PROCESS

The planning process starts with identifying your current address and outlining the steps you'll need to take in order to get you to your desired destination. This is where you determine the time it will take, the resources you will need, the people with expertise who can help you, and how you will overcome the obstacles. This is one of my favorite parts of the AUDIT Principle. I love to help people chart their course and come up with their own unique plan for success.

I remember sitting around the dining room table with my parents the night after reading my teacher's journal comments. That night, with the help of my parents, we wrote out a simple plan based on the steps I would have to take in order to become a doctor. We started with the end in mind and then listed each requirement we knew was going to be necessary to becoming a doctor.

For example, becoming a doctor would require a bachelor's degree with an emphasis in math and science. Next, I would have to get accepted into medical school. And finally, I would have to figure out a way to pay for it all. The timetable was an important ingredient to consider as well. It would take eight or more years just to become a doctor, not to mention the additional time it would take to build a successful practice.

Once we identified the obvious requirements, my parents led me deeper into the process of imagining and planning. Together, we acknowledged the fact that medical school would be tough to get into and that I would need excellent grades from a four-year college. I would also need an exceptional resume, as well as letters of recommendation from people with influence.

We acknowledged that I didn't have much to work with. We couldn't ignore the fact that my poor academic history had already automatically disqualified me from step one, which was admittance into most four-year colleges. Also, I didn't have a positive resume or know people of influence who could recommend me. To say I had some obvious limitations right out of the starting gate is an understatement!

But this is where the power and "magic" of the business plan comes into play. Creating a plan removes the excuses and the emotion attached to them. The plan simply identifies the end destination, acknowledges the starting point, and requires that you think through the steps, requirements and finances that must happen in order to get you to your finish line.

WRITING DOWN YOUR PLAN

Although it would require further research and some professional advice to complete, that night my parents and I wrote out a simple and straightforward plan. It went something like this:

YEAR ONE: Enroll in a local community college. Take remedial classes in math and science in order to build critical new learning skills and acquire a new, higher grade point average.

YEARS TWO - FOUR: Transfer to a local four-year college where I can still live at home to save money. Maintain a steady job to earn an income.

YEARS ONE - FOUR: Volunteer in extracurricular activities in order to build relationships and a strong resume, and to "try out" new jobs that could lead to higher pay.

YEARS FOUR - EIGHT: Apply, get accepted, and attend medical school.

I would also need to conduct some research and get outside direction from advisers. It was critical for me to form new relationships with college entrance counselors, financial aid advisers, and others who could help me along my way. There were other details to pursue and points to consider, but for the most part, my plan was conceived that night around the kitchen table with my parents.

I followed that plan for five full years before deciding it was going to be necessary to change vehicles. Following the plan moved me toward my destination while expanding my skills, relationships, and opportunities. It kept me from straying too far away from my destination.

Ultimately, I didn't become a doctor, but I did end up with a career in the health care industry. My early efforts were not wasted. I discovered insurance was a vehicle that suited me much better than a medical practice. Even though the vehicle changed, the plan kept me moving toward my goal, dream, and destination. All of this was possible because I understood that my career choice wasn't the destination; it was merely the vehicle.

Until I started a company of my own, I had never been involved in raising capital and I didn't know how to read financial statements. In fact, I didn't have many of the other critical skills that common sense says every CEO ought to possess. But my past had taught me an important principle: "As long as I have a plan, I can follow it. And if there are tasks within the plan that I can't personally execute, I can hire someone else to do it for me. Just give me a map that's easy to read with enough detail and guideposts along the way, and I know I can get to my destination." The same principle holds true with any good plan.

There are many schools of thought that debate the value of a plan. Some suggest that you only need a plan if you are going to raise capital. Others believe that you need to hire an outside firm of consultants to construct a glossy and highly detailed report. But that's not been my experience. My advice is to keep it simple. Resist the temptation to get too much into the details.

Just write out the plan of what you want to do. Describe your venture, its purpose, strategy, and location. Describe how you plan to start, what you believe will be your hurdles and solutions, and who will be involved. Don't forget to include a timeline with significant benchmarks and sound financial projections.

A GOOD PLAN IS COMMON SENSE

Before taking a vacation, you create a plan that includes a map and takes into consideration basic information like the weather conditions, how much time you have, and how much money you have to spend. Before you leave, a plan shows you the purpose of your trip, where you are starting from, and where you are going.

Before building your dream house, you create a blueprint of the finished home. Not only is a blueprint important for making sure you'll be able to meet your family's needs and desires, but you also need it to direct your builders and vendors. Your blueprint is an important requirement to bring you into compliance with local legal codes.

Every good plan contains sound financial projections made with the expertise of a good financial adviser. My brother Bob articulates this principle well: "There have been a number of times when, as a CPA, I have looked at a business that was failing and have had to ask the difficult question. 'What were you thinking?' To the trained eye, it seems obvious, but the average person just doesn't see it."

That Memorial Day weekend, Bob and I were each working on our own portions of the business plan. I was writing the company description, the organizational structure, and other narratives, while my brother worked on one-year, three-year, and five-year financial projections for our company. With the information from the financial projections, we knew exactly how much money we needed to raise in order to start the business, rent an office space, hire our first employee, and even how much we'd need to begin paying me a salary.

A plan also helps to address and compensate for any deficiencies or weaknesses you might have. For example, because of my weaknesses in accounting, I knew I was going to have to surround myself with financial advisers that would implement strong financial processes and controls. As a result of these key steps in my plan, my weaknesses actually served to make us stronger than many startup companies.

You have your own important decisions to make as you work your way through this process. Ask yourself, What's my destination, where do I want to be? What kind of vehicle will I need to get there? The answers to these important questions will help you create a plan of your own. Now it's time to use your imagination!

SEE IT THROUGH

ONCE YOU'VE **Assessed** your current address and you've come to an **Understanding** of your destination, made some critical **Decisions** and **Imagined** your plan, you're ready for the fifth and final step of the AUDIT Principle.

Commit yourself fully to the process. You have to **See it Through!** All your hard work up to this point will be wasted unless you're prepared to see it all the way through to the very end. Lots of people start. Far fewer people finish.

One of the most common reasons that businesses fail or that people never achieve their dreams is because they give up before reaching the finish line. It seems that almost every time I encounter someone who's not been able to achieve their goals, dreams, or visions, it's because they stopped short of the finish line.

Most people aren't committed to seeing it all the way through to the end. So much potential is left unrealized. I once heard it said that it's amazing how much wealth is buried in every graveyard just because people gave up before finishing their race. Who knows how much greatness we'd all be capable of if we didn't quit too early? You always have the chance to succeed until you quit.

Finishing your race strong might sound like an over-simplification, but its importance can't be minimized. At the start, everyone wants to finish. There's all this energy and excitement. Anything is possible; finishing seems like a slam-dunk certainty. But when the going gets tough, only those who are committed to finishing will actually do it. Right at the start, when your energy level is at its highest, you need to make the commitment that you are going to see it through, and then see it through no matter what!

Never forget that committing to any kind of project is an adventure. The dictionary tells us that an adventure is a bold and risky undertaking. So, by definition, any journey or venture worth pursuing is going to have its share of challenges. Your journey will be no different. If it were easy to lose weight or start a company or run a marathon, everyone would be doing it.

But it's not easy. Weariness, Hopelessness, Despair, and Frustration will all be traveling companions along your way. There will be times you'll struggle with deep disappointment or frustration when things don't work out. At some point along the way, you'll likely run out of money or time or other resources. That's the nature of these things. We all get blindsided. But those are times when you have to set your emotions aside and press through. Remind yourself that all adventures are full of challenges. That's what makes them adventures!

STIR UP YOUR FAITH

In the early years of my company, I don't think a week went by that my brother didn't call to tell me that if I didn't do something significant, we were going to run out of money and have to close our doors. I didn't qualify for bank loans and I'd already gone to my shareholders so much they were tapped out. I remember many times sitting at my desk mired in hopelessness.

Of course, I did my best not to communicate my hopelessness to Bob. I would immediately tell him not to worry and I'd assure him that I would find the money. Then I'd shake off my discouragement and get down to business. I'd do what needed to be done. I'd start making phone calls and knocking on doors.

I did my best not to entertain discouraging or negative emotions or thoughts. Instead, I'd stir up my faith. As quick as I recognized hopelessness, despair, frustration, or discouragement, I would replace those negative thoughts with positive declarations and rehearse our prior successes. In doing that one simple exercise, I found that I could renew my thinking. It helped turn the switch from negative to positive.

Any big goal, venture, or dream will be challenging. There's a good chance that your venture will take longer and cost more than you think it will. There will be lots of times when you'll want to throw in the towel and call it quits.

As with most adventures, you get through those times with the support of guides, advisers, coaches, and mentors. The trained adventure guide who is skilled and experienced on a river knows where the dangerous rocks are hiding and helps you to avoid them, navigating through the white water. Or the coach or mentor who can teach technique corrects and pushes you further than you thought you could go.

IT'S NOT ABOUT YOU

One of the most powerful motivators for seeing it through all the way to the end is to realize that your success in this venture is not just about you. There are others in this with you, and they are relying on you to be successful. If you're not successful, they won't be either.

Chances are, you'll have employees who depend on you for their paycheck, family members who are depending on you to provide for them, shareholders who are looking for a return on their investment, donors who depend on your wise use of their donations, and even vendors who depend on the business you swing their way. In short, you have a community of people who all, in many ways, are dependent on you seeing this through and not quitting.

It's as if you were running a marathon through the city streets lined with a crowd cheering you on. But in this case, the crowd is made up of both people you know and don't know, all dependent on your success. They are all pulling for you to finish. Being successful allows you to be generous with your time, influence and resources. Your success, or lack of it, affects many people. This image alone should be a powerful fuel for endurance.

In my case, it was very clear to me that the success of our company didn't rely entirely on me. I understood that the solution to every problem was found in God and in the relationships I had formed, both new and existing. I understood what my role was, which was to keep making the calls and knocking on doors until we had the money.

The same is true in your case. Your dream is growing inside you, and it's your responsibility to see it through, giving birth to that dream once it matures. But you are not in this alone. You are supported in your efforts by all those people you've been able to share your dream with. They surround you and ensure your success.

The strategic relationships you've been able to forge along the way will always prove to be your greatest asset. There is no challenge, question, or problem that cannot be solved through a relationship. Whether you need finances, influence, skills, or access, they will all be found in the relationships you form.

The greatest strategy, in life or in business, is to build, cultivate, and honor your relationships. This strategy and principle was demonstrated in each stage of my company's development, from raising capital to hiring employees and selecting vendors, from meeting clients to building a support network that, in many ways, has turned into lifelong friendships.

Challenging times always make for great stories *after* you've gone through the challenge! Going through them is no fun. But once you've seen it through and come out the other side, you'll have enough stories to write a book of your own!

Once you've made the commitment to see it through to the end, quitting is not an option. You'll just naturally look for a way to move forward. And the more forward steps you take, the more your confidence will build. You'll come to think that no matter how bad it might get, you'll always be able to find the right solution for any situation that might present itself.

We all know that we don't learn the valuable lessons of life by going through the easy times. It's the difficult times that teach us the most. The difficult times ahead will be the places where you'll develop the skills, strengths, influence, and reputation that will be invaluable when you start your next venture.

SEARCHING FOR THE KEYS

The phrase "searching for the keys" became a popular saying in my company. It meant to push forward and not give up, to see it through and keep searching for the keys until you find them. Finish!

The phrase comes from a story from my high school years. I had a friend named Bobby who was always getting in trouble. Of course, every incident became a great story that we couldn't wait to share with one another. One night Bobby took a young lady to the beach on the Balboa Peninsula. This beach stretches several miles up the coast of Southern California.

About 11:30 that night, he walked the young lady back to the car, probably a mile or so from where they'd been hanging out. He had to get her home before her midnight curfew. When they got back to the car, Bobby reached into his pocket for his car keys and couldn't find them. He checked and double-checked every pocket and no luck. He finally realized that he must have lost them somewhere along that stretch of beach. Of course, he had no idea where.

They started to look for the keys but knew there was no

way they'd be able to find them before the curfew, and he had to get this poor girl home. In desperation, he made the call none of us wants to make: he called his mom. You can imagine how furious his mom was. But she agreed to come and meet them at his car.

When she got there, she gave Bobby the keys to her own car so he could get the young lady home before curfew, then she started off toward the stretch of sand with her rake and a flashlight. Her plan was to find the keys and then drive back home in Bobby's car. She was confident and, with no Plan B, determined to keep searching until she found those keys. Those keys represented her only way home.

Throughout that night and into the early morning, by the light of the moon and her trusty flashlight, Bobby's mom raked that sand from the parking lot to the spot where Bobby said he'd been. She raked and raked until she found those keys!

I never forgot that story, and it's always encouraged me to keep pushing forward, to "keep raking the sand" no matter what. Whenever I felt desperate and needed additional resources or more clients or creative solutions and felt like giving up, I always pictured Bobby's mom on the beach in the middle of the night, tenaciously searching for those keys in a sea of sand.

KEEP YOUR EYE ON THE PRIZE

To be effective in seeing it through, you must be able to keep your eye on the prize. You need to constantly keep a vision of the finish line in front of you. Do whatever you've got to do to give yourself daily reminders of why you are pursuing this, why you're working so hard, and why it's so important to finish.

When I owned my company, I practiced a daily ritual until I was able to sell the companies. My husband Mark bought a box of those little paper umbrellas they put in your drink when you're vacationing in tropical locations and made sure one of them was in every drink I had at home. He would also find a way to get those umbrellas in my drinks when we traveled together. He even made sure my employees did the same thing for me at the office. Every time I had a soda or even a glass of water, it would come with a little colorful umbrella in it.

All of my dreams would rush through my mind whenever I saw one of those silly umbrellas in my drink. To me, the umbrella reminded me of relaxing on the beach, and that simple symbol began to represent the goal of selling my company. This one tangible way kept my eye on the prize so I could see it through. That's how powerful keeping your vision in front of you can be!

Keeping your vision in front of you, in one form or another, is critical. It's a daily reminder of what you are working so hard for. Several months after David died, I felt that I needed to sell our home and buy a new one. It wasn't that there was anything particularly wrong with the old home, except it now represented the past for me. It was important for me to find a new house, a new place that would inhabit my future. I felt that this would be one important way for me to move on.

The day I bought the new house, I had a vision of another

new house, a dream home for the future. I pictured a house in a specific area of town on a large lot surrounded by deer with a river running through it. I had never been in that part of town before, but I had heard a lot about it and formed a picture of it in my mind. Over the next fifteen years, I dreamed about this home and talked about it to others.

The week before my company sold, I was ready to buy my new home. I called a real estate agent and told her what I wanted and where I wanted to look. As we drove through the neighborhood looking at houses, we passed a beautiful home with six deer peacefully grazing in the front yard. I knew that was going to be my new home.

Today, I'm living in that home on the beautiful lot. In fact, as I write this paragraph, I can look out my window and see two bucks and several does lying out beyond our pond. This view is a constant reminder to me of how important it is to keep your vision in front of you. It will keep you moving in the right direction.

Another example of a big dream connected to successfully selling the companies was the exciting privilege of donating a large sum of money to charitable causes. I envisioned exactly how I would give the gifts and which organizations I would give them to. Once the acquisition of my companies took place, I made those visions a reality. The first checks I wrote were donations to the organizations I'd imagined.

Keeping your vision in front of you is powerful. It will inspire you to accomplish much for yourself and can help you discover the joy of helping others too.

LESSONS FROM THE HOSPITAL

Throughout the eight months of fighting David's battle with cancer, my faith and commitment to seeing it through were challenged in ways I could never have imagined. I felt like I was in the middle of the biggest fight of my faith and life. The last seven days in the hospital were especially difficult.

I only left David's bedside long enough for short trips home to shower and clean up. The one time I made an exception was to go down to the hospital chapel to pray. Little did I know I would have a God-encounter that would build my confidence and help me see things through.

It was six nights into my hospital vigil, and I was tired and frightened. David's vital signs were weakening, and I was struggling to hold on to my hope.

As I rode the elevator down to the chapel that night, I caught myself thinking the same words that I had prayed years earlier when I was fighting another battle. *God, either you are or you're not, and if you are*—I was about to say, "Then you are everything you say you are and you need to heal David," when my thoughts were completely stopped, and I heard a different thought in my head.

No, Jane Ann, we established who I am a long time ago. But are you who you say you are?

The elevator doors opened, and I made my way to the chapel with profound confidence that God was who He said He was, but I needed to ask myself some difficult questions. I went to the front and got down on my knees. I poured over the following questions:

- Regardless of the outcome, would I still be committed to be the best mom possible to my son?

- Would I remain present and engaged, committed to giving my son a full and happy life?

- Would I allow the current disappointment and grief I felt to derail me, or would I pursue the dreams and goals that continued to live inside me?

That night I decided that despite the outcome, despite my feelings and the challenges I knew would come, I would spend my life working to become all I could be.

Every decision matters. There are lots of people depending on you to succeed. So step up to the starting line and be prepared to go all the way. You've got lots of people cheering you on to become all you can be, to live a fully empowered and abundant life. When you can do that, not only will you achieve your goal of arriving at your destination, but all those around you will benefit too, all because you were committed to seeing it through.

Commit to finish strong and become all you can be. Hold fast to the plan you made at the start and see it through until you cross the finish line.

CONCLUSION

I T'S COMMON TO HEAR THE PHRASE, "Sometimes we have to hit bottom before we can begin to rise." Although I believe this adage has proven to be true for many of us at different seasons of our lives, it's not the ideal way to bring about change. Change can begin as soon as you recognize that your actions no longer support your values, your purpose, your goals and dreams.

Over the years I've had plenty of opportunities to study the lives of others as well as my own. As a result of that study, I've discovered that every life is a great story and includes its share of challenges, obstacles, and successes. All of these things work together to test our faith and endurance while developing resilience, resolve, and the ability to live out an amazing destiny.

The challenges, suffering, confusion, dissatisfaction, and disillusionment aren't prejudiced. They affect all of us, regardless of our socio-economic position, religion, or gender. They affect us both in the challenges and tragedies we face as well as in the successes we experience.

What sets us apart, of course, is how we respond. It's in our response, and the decisions that follow, that determine whether or not we are going to rise above the struggles or allow them to drag us under. It's in those defining moments that our greatness emerges, presenting us with opportunities to make life-changing choices that, when aligned with appropriate strategies, result in unlimited possibilities.

If we have determined what our goals are and supported those goals with purpose and correct strategies, following through with actions that are aligned with those strategies, we can expect to experience results, possibly beyond what we were aiming for.

Add to that a written plan that allows a community of like-minded people to follow and support us in our pursuit of our goals and dreams, and there is nothing we can't accomplish. Unless we get weary, give up, and fail to see it through.

When you fail to live intentionally with purpose, strategy and goals, it always leads, regretfully and predictably, to your dreams going unfulfilled. On the other hand, you can live life with a predictable and expected outcome when you commit to living motivated by purpose and timely goals.

It is my supposition that we've been placed on Planet Earth in order to live life to the fullest, contributing to the well-being and improvement of the current and future generations. We do this by making important choices with intention. This was the genesis and remains the basis for the AUDIT Principle. Although it's not always easy to follow, it is a simple blueprint to living well.

Choosing to implement the AUDIT Principle is choosing

to take responsibility for your life and its outcomes. It's a decision to assess your current status, acknowledging those things you have at your disposal and the things you don't. It's a realistic look at your current position in relationship to where you ultimately want to be, your desired outcome.

Choosing to follow this Principle is doing whatever it takes to better understand your desired outcome or the destination you are striving for, then making the steadfast decision to eliminate denial, excuses, or blame. It's claiming your responsibility and power to pursue and achieve your goals, dreams and visions. It's stepping forward and accepting your call to a destiny like it proclaims in Luke 12:48: "To whom much is given, much is required."

Following the AUDIT Principle is making the decision that you will go for it, that you will not quit or give up, that you'll pursue it all the way to the end. The AUDIT Principle recognizes the only way you can fail is to give up and stop pursuing your dreams. It's imagining the blueprint to success, the road map that will get you to your destination.

The AUDIT Principle will help you live a life of purpose and intention. It will help you align your actions with the goals you want to achieve. It will help you identify the hurdles and distractions in your path so you can put strategies in place that will help you deal with them. The AUDIT Principle gives you a path to follow, as well as a guide to lead you along your journey to success. The AUDIT Principle provides a simple five-step plan that will help you live the life you were born to live!

ACKNOWLEDGMENTS

THROUGHOUT MY LIFE I've been surrounded and blessed with teachers, pastors, bosses and mentors who have believed and invested in me. Each of you have played a significant role in my life. You are a big part of the story behind *The AUDIT Principle*. Thank you.

Every project and success I've experienced has happened because of the dedication, talent, and contribution of my colleagues, partners, investors, and employees. Life and business have been a great adventure because of the role each of you have played. Thank you.

Writing this book couldn't have happened without the team of experts who came along side of me at just the right time. Thank you, John Mason and Michael Staires at Insight International, for two years of collaborating with me on *The AUDIT Principle*. Thank you to Scott Spiewak at Fresh Impact for your unwavering encouragement, support, and friendship, and Francine Platt at Eden Graphics for your creativity, talent and late nights in bringing *The AUDIT Principle* to life. Thank you, Jodi Orgill Brown, for your inspiration, friendship, and help in getting this book to print.

Special thanks to my husband Mark, and to family and friends who have encouraged and stood with me through the remarkable journey of writing *The AUDIT Principle*.

And to my favorite passage, Proverbs 3:6, that led me to where I am today: "In all thy ways acknowledge Him, and He shall direct thy paths."

ABOUT THE AUTHOR

Jane Ann Craig is a motivational speaker, entrepreneur, and author. She is passionate in sharing her powerful message about how people and organizations can and should achieve success beyond their own goals and dreams.

Her life is an inspiring story. It proves that even when we are most challenged, we can rise above our circumstances and achieve extraordinary success.

Upon becoming a widow and the sole provider of her two-year-old son, Jane Ann started a multimillion-dollar organization, ultimately selling it to a multibillion-dollar company. She has helped train, mentor, and launch countless professional and executive careers.

For more information about the author, visit www.janeanncraig.com

Made in the USA
Lexington, KY
01 October 2018